THE DESERT

RDB

THE DESERT

RUSSELL D. BUTCHER

Introduction by Morris K. Udall
Member, U.S. House of Representatives

A Studio Book · The Viking Press · New York

Other books by Russell D. Butcher:
MAINE PARADISE
NEW MEXICO

Excerpt from the editorial, "Fragile beauty," May 19, 1972, is
reprinted by permission from *The Christian Science Monitor*. ©
1972 The Christian Science Publishing Society. All rights reserved.

Text and black-and-white photographs Copyright © 1976
by Russell D. Butcher and Pamela R. Butcher
Color photographs copyright in all countries of the International
Copyright Union 1976 by Russell D. Butcher and Pamela R. Butcher
All rights reserved
First published in 1976 by The Viking Press, Inc.
625 Madison Avenue, New York, N.Y. 10022
Published simultaneously in Canada by
The Macmillan Company of Canada Limited
Text and black-and-white photographs printed in U.S.A.
Color photographs printed in Japan by Dai Nippon

Library of Congress Cataloging in Publication Data

Butcher, Russell D
  The desert.
  (A Studio book)
  Bibliography: p.
  1. Desert biology—United States. 2. Deserts—
United States. I. Title.
QH104.B88   500.9′78   75–42307
ISBN 0-670-26712-0

Contents

Dedicated to all true "Desert Rats"

To those who come to the desert with tolerance it gives friendliness; to those who come
with courage it gives new strength of character. . . . For those seeking beauty the desert
offers nature's rarest artistry.

—Randall Henderson
On Desert Trails

Acknowledgments

My dear wife, Pam, has been a full partner in nearly every phase of this book—on the many
inspiring field trips, in editing and typing the manuscript, and in scores of other ways. To her my
loving thanks—most of all for her own deep love of the desert, and for her constant faith that such a
book would become a reality.

I am deeply grateful to Mo Udall for his contribution to this book, reflecting his own commitment
to the protection of the environment.

For many kindnesses and for the use of their two photographs, I owe a debt of thanks to our good
friends, Drs. Walter R. and Sally Hoyt Spofford. Thanks also to Dr. Vince D. Roth, resident director
of the American Museum of Natural History's Southwestern Research Station, Portal, Arizona; to
Joseph F. Carithers, superintendent of Big Bend National Park, Texas; and to our good friends of
"Marty-Dess" Photo Service, Douglas, Arizona.

Finally, a special word of thanks to my parents, Mary and Devereux Butcher, who encouraged me
to see and value the beauty of nature.

Introduction

A century ago, few Americans would have looked twice at a photographic study of America's deserts. To our ancestors, a land that could not be dominated by man was a land to be ignored. The very word "desert" called forth images of endless bleakness, an oppressive lifelessness.

To be sure, some American deserts fit the conception of silent, lifeless basins or whispering sands. But other lands called "desert" teem with a fantastic spectrum of animal and plant species, each adapted to the special demands of arid, unsheltered life.

Russ Butcher's photography and text capture this incredible variety of rugged life systems—from the sunken stillness of Death Valley to the panoramic majesty of Monument Valley to the rich beauty of my home, the Sonoran Desert of southern Arizona.

Man has lived in our deserts for thousands of years. More and more, however, we need to know whether he can live *with* the desert. Each day's headlines add credence to the proposition that there are limits to our ability to change our environment, for such changes require massive commitments of resources that are becoming ever more scarce, while worldwide demand for them swells.

To those of us who have lived in deserts most of our lives—I was born on the steppes of northern Arizona and since reaching adulthood have lived in the Sonoran Desert—these developments have a special significance. We have watched the population of our desert regions grow at a fantastic rate; my home town has grown from 50,000 people before World War II to half a million today. This human tide shows little sign of abatement. Indeed, the spiraling costs of energy make the warmth of desert regions all the more attractive to millions.

As more and more people move West, the demands on scarce resources will grow. More land for new homes, more water from already depleted sources, and more fuel to accommodate the mobile lifestyle of the "wide open spaces"—all will be demanded. Yet today we are learning that these resources are finite and that we are nearing the limit in exploiting them. The desert, with its limited rainfall, is easily disrupted and slow to recover.

Overgrazing of cattle strips the sparse vegetation from our hills, causing ruinous erosion during the brief torrential storms that characterize our rainy season.

Urban and agricultural demands deplete our deep ground-water reserves, while the spread of construction and channelization projects keeps our limited rainfall from sinking into the earth to replenish the aquifer.

The age of the offroad vehicle, while giving new access to many for responsible use of the desert, has enabled a few vandals to reach remote sites where rare animals are slaughtered and a priceless archaeological heritage is looted or defaced.

In my fourteen years in Congress, we have made great strides toward protecting this special resource. National parks, monuments, and forests preserve many of the most spectacular desert sites, some developed for recreation and education, others left in their natural state as parts of the wilderness system.

Even more promising is a new legislative effort. As this book goes to press, Congress is considering a historic new program for the management of additional desert areas in the public domain—a system of Desert Conservation Areas under the jurisdiction of the Bureau of Land Management. This proposal would enable the federal government to coordinate the many potential uses of our deserts: recreation, archaeology, education, mineral development, the preservation of rare flora and fauna. Perhaps those who read this book and meet the desert's splendor for the first time will begin to understand the special attachment I feel for what some call wastelands, and perhaps they will help us move forward in this critically needed effort.

These pages portray, in photographs and words, the majesty and infinite variety of lands we call desert, the ways plants and animals adapt to extremes of heat and dryness. For man, accustomed to bringing nature under his dominion, it is at once a humbling and uplifting environment—humbling because the hardness of the land and the vestiges of forgotten civilizations scratched upon its surface remind him of his own mortality; uplifting because in the solitude of these vast spaces he can gain new insight into himself and his relationship to the world.

MORRIS K. UDALL

Foreword

Vast uncluttered spaces of solitude and far horizons, the deserts of the West extend uninterrupted from west Texas to southern California, and north to eastern Oregon. They are sun-baked and arid; vegetation does not smother the land—each plant stands, individual and separate, on its own piece of stony or sandy ground. Never are you out of sight of boldly jutting mountain ranges, some of starkly eroded rock, others rising like islands into cool green forests.

In these six great deserts you can see the earth itself, sense how it has been created over aeons by immense pressures from within and sculptured by wind and rain. You begin to grasp that man is witness to only the barest moment of onflowing changes of topography, climate, and life itself.

Yet not everything in the deserts is on so vast a scale of place and time. There are the details, the plants and animals that have adapted themselves in a thousand different ways to the extremes of drought and burning sun. From cactus to sagebrush and from rattlesnakes to desert bighorn sheep, each has evolved and perfected its own way of thriving in the hostile environment.

To many people, the desert seems only a barren wasteland, a terrifyingly empty land of crushing heat, venomous reptiles, and thorny plant life—a place that is best scurried across on a four-lane freeway on the way to somewhere else.

But for a growing number of others, the subtropical and rain-shadow deserts of the West are endlessly fascinating environments—where the slanting sun of early morning and late afternoon accentuates the colors and textures of the land, the songs of birds fill the air, masses of brilliant spring wildflowers carpet the ground, and the brightest canopy of stars moves across the sky at night.

As Randall Henderson, founder of *Desert* magazine, wrote in *On Desert Trails,* "the real desert . . . is not for the eyes of the superficial observer or the fearful soul of a cynic. It is a land which reveals its true character only to those who come with courage, tolerance, and understanding."

It is my hope that the photographs and text of this book, portraying some of the outstanding and most accessible desert places, will help to inspire a deeper understanding of the beauty and meaning of the deserts.

R. D. B.
Portal, Arizona

Border Country

The Chihuahuan Desert

Along the Mexican border of west Texas, the Rio Grande makes a great swing southward. Cupped in the river's curve lies a wild and arid desert, where for millions of years the river's muddy waters have been carving awesome canyons through gigantic limestone plateaus and crumpled mountain ranges. In its center the craggy, castle-like summits of the Chisos Mountains jut up thousands of feet, dominating remoteness and endless distances of the desert. This is the Big Bend country of the Chihuahuan Desert, where the plains end and the great western deserts begin.

Emerging from a thicket of mesquite and tamarisk, the trail to Santa Elena Canyon crosses the sandy floodplain of Terlingua Creek. Straight ahead rises Mesa de Anguila, its imposing 1500-foot-high sheer escarpment sliced by the immense gorge of the Rio Grande.

The top of the switchbacking trail into the canyon's mouth provides a spectacular view upstream. Brilliant morning sunlight floods the north wall, while across the wide, silt-laden river the cliffs in Mexico, rising straight from the water's edge, are in dark shadow.

Dense stands of tall, bamboo-like reed grass and the feathery foliage of tamarisk provide a band of tropical lush green along the riverbank. Great angular boulders lie scattered here and there where they have crashed down from the cliffs above.

In spring the canyon echoes back and forth with the enthusiastic, down-trilling song of the little canyon wren and the "wichity-wichity-wichity" of the yellowthroat, a tiny yellow-and-olive warbler with a black face mask. Chittering white-throated swifts endlessly swoop and circle overhead in acrobatic pursuit of insects.

As the trail leads farther into Santa Elena, it appears that the river is running downhill at a steeper angle than it actually is. But this is an optical illusion, caused by the tilting dip of the layered rock strata.

These massive formations of limestone were slowly laid down beneath a shallow arm of the sea more than a hundred million years ago, during the age of the dinosaurs. Aeons later tremendous pressures within the earth caused immense chunks of the land to drop down, while others were forced upward. When the great river encountered these gradually uplifting blocks of the earth, it slowly began to grind through them. For seventeen miles the mighty power of water and silt has carved this winding route, forming in its lower stretch a deeply incised canyon in the highest side of the uptilted mesa.

Although the trail into the shaded depths of the canyon ends abruptly at the water's edge less than a mile from the end of the road, it really seems as though you had traveled a thousand miles from civilization and far back in time. The silent elemental surging river and the grand architecture of the sculptured walls close around conspire to lift the human mind into hushed awe.

The Rio Grande has carved two other great gorges on its 107-mile swing along the southern edge of Big Bend National Park. Mariscal, midway along the river's course, is the deepest (1600 feet), the shortest (seven miles), and the most popular with river-runners on single-day float trips.

Boquillas Canyon, at the far eastern end of the park, is a spectacular twenty-three-mile gash through the Sierra del Carmen. Unlike the other two gorges, Boquillas is wider, has many intriguing side canyons to explore, and no tricky rockfalls, like those of Santa Elena, to navigate or portage.

A short distance upstream from the towering yellowish cliffs at the mouth of Boquillas Canyon lies a level stretch of river floodplain, inviting in late autumn, winter, and early spring, before the low country becomes oppressively hot.

Springtime, when the groves of fragrant honey and screw-bean mesquites (*Prosopis juliflora* and *Prosopis pubescens*) are in full bloom, is the best time to see and hear many kinds of low-desert birds along the river. There are the bright red cardinals and rose-pink-and-gray cardinal-like pyrrhuloxias, the persistently cooing white-winged doves that seem to say "who-cooks-for-you?", tiny verdins, mockingbirds, and vibrant vermilion flycatchers and summer tanagers. The comical long-tailed road-runner, a ground cuckoo, dashes in hot pursuit of lizards.

Darkness brings out gray foxes, coyotes, raccoons, and tiny long-tailed kangaroo rats. Families of collared peccaries, or javelinas (*Pecari angulatus*), a hairy, piglike animal, wander about in early morning or late afternoon. Their strange grunts and snarls can be heard at night, as they tear at agave leaves or cactus pads.

There may be the exuberant, frantic "ee-ah-ing" of burros across the river. A happy Mexican melodiously sings his heart out in the hush of evening. Along a little strip of sandy beach, next to a rustling stand of tall reed grass, the river's calm surface reflects the sun's last orange and pink glow that has set ablaze the high, banded escarpment of Mexico's Sierra del Carmen.

On a windy October day we watched a long wave of cloud spill over the brink of Sierra del Carmen. Halfway down the face of the long escarpment the cloud's lower edge dissipated as it came in contact with the warm, dry air of the desert. It was like a giant wave of water frozen in mid-air. The dramatic spectacle lasted for hours.

Vast expanses between the lush growth by the river and the pine-and-oak woodlands of the high Chisos Mountains are sparsely covered with desert plant life. Although lacking the distinctive saguaro and organ-pipe cacti of the Arizona–Sonoran Desert or the weirdly branching Joshua tree of the Mojave Desert, this part of the Chihuahuan Desert nevertheless supports a tremendous variety of fascinating and beautiful plants.

A prolific, small species of century plant, known as lechuguilla (*Agave lechuguilla*), with a tall, narrow spike of purplish or yellow flowers, thickly covers vast stretches of the ground. In many places it is virtually impossible to walk because of the dense growth of the sharply barbed, curved, swordlike leaves. A member of the pineapple family, called false agave (*Hechtia scariosa*), covers some of the low-elevation limestone ridges. The abundant creosote bush (*Larrea tridentata*), whose upward fanning olive-green shrubs bloom in spring with tiny yellow flowers, is a familiar sight. Tarbush (*Flourensia cernua*), another common evergreen shrub with small yellow flowers, is one of the key floral indicators of the Chihuahuan Desert.

Graceful "forests" of ocotillo, or coachwhip (*Fouquieria splendens*), range from Texas to California. Its slender, thorn-covered stems or canes fan upward twelve, fifteen, or even twenty-five feet. Much of the year it is dormant, appearing gray and lifeless, but after sufficient rains soak the land, its stems become thickly covered with tiny bright green leaves. When the heat and drought return, the leaves turn yellow or brown and fall off. New leaves have been known to appear, in some desert areas and in times of exceptional moisture, as many as three or four times in a year. In late spring and early summer the ocotillo bursts into bloom with a brilliant red or reddish-orange panicle of flowers at the end of each stem. When hundreds of these plants fill a sweep of the land with touches of vibrant color, it is one of the desert's most beautiful displays.

Many varieties of cacti also brighten the Big Bend country during spring and summer: brilliant yellow, waxy-looking blossoms of prickly pear and giant fishhook cacti; magenta, pink, and orange kinds of rainbow hedgehog; reddish-maroon rattail; dazzling pinkish-red strawberry and eagle's-claw; magenta-purple cane cholla and pink cory-cactus; and the rich orange-red claret-cup.

Desert fragrances are rich and unique. One late afternoon, as we headed up the road toward the Chisos, a thunderstorm pounded great slashing bolts of lightning onto the jagged peaks and emptied a dark curtain of rain from its billowing thunderhead. As the storm moved over us, we smelled a pungent aroma associated only with the deserts of the Southwest—the refreshing fragrance of rain-washed creosote bush.

At the upper edge of the desert a transition zone of desert grassland extends into the base of the mountains. Mule deer, desert cottontail, the little "cotton-top" scaled quail, and, in late spring, the striking yellow-and-black Scott's orioles are especially abundant there.

Dotted across the grasslands are sotol (*Dasylirion leiophyllum*), nolina or basket grass (*Nolina erumpens*), and several kinds of yuccas. All are distinctive members of the lily family and produce clumps of long, narrow leaves, out of which grow tall florescences of creamy-white flowers. Companion to these is the giant-stalked maguey (*Agave scabra*). This huge century plant gradually enlarges its clump of grayish-green, dagger-sharp basal leaves, over a period of ten to fifteen years. Then suddenly one summer it quickly produces a stalk up to fifteen feet tall, upon which are festooned as many as twenty branches bearing clusters of golden flowers. Even while the maguey blossoms are attracting insects and hummingbirds to their nectar, the basal leaves begin to turn brown, prelude to death, for the plant has expended all its stored food on this ultimate floral triumph.

Not so with the yuccas. They will put out their showy whitish flowers year after year, some years more than others. Big Bend's most spectacular yucca display is at Dagger Flat when the giant daggers (*Yucca carnerosana*) come into bloom from March to June. Some are more than twenty feet tall, boasting single stalks with hundreds, perhaps a thousand, bell-shaped white blossoms.

Rising above the desert and desert grassland expanses, the rugged Chisos Mountains are the prominent centerpiece of the landscape. They also encompass a whole range of dramatically different life zones of flora and fauna that are caused by a decrease in temperature and an increase of rainfall. It is really a "sky island" amid the vast sea of surrounding desert.

The Chisos are an unusual overlapping point for some typically Mexican plants and animals that range into few or no other places in the United States, and for other plants of more northerly regions of the West that reach their southernmost point there. Douglas firs, ponderosa pines, and quaking aspens grow in some of the cooler canyons and at higher elevations—isolated outposts of species that were apparently more widespread throughout this region during the wetter, cooler Ice Age thousands of years ago. Coming across from Mexico is the beautiful drooping juniper (*Juniperus flaccida*). Also from Mexico, the little rufous-crowned Colima warbler (*Vermivora crissalis*) breeds in hidden places in these mountains, notably in Boot Canyon.

The rugged peaks of the Chisos are the product of an often violent mountain-building period of roughly ten to sixty million years ago. The oldest of the rocks consist of such materials as volcanic tuff (compacted ash), sandstone, conglomerates, and thick remnants of lava flows that cap some of the higher summits. It was during this period that mammals were gradually replacing the reptiles, including the great dinosaurs, as the dominant life forms on earth. Among the new creatures were early species of camels, horses, tapirs, a rhinoceros, a hippopotamus-like animal, and a panther-like cat—all now extinct.

One of the world's most exciting fossil finds of modern times, made recently at Big Bend, was the discovery of three partial skeletons of a long-extinct species of winged reptile called a pterosaur, or pterodactyl, which lived during the late Cretaceous period, toward the end of the age of the dinosaurs some sixty-five million years ago. The wingspan of the Big Bend pterosaur was somewhere between forty and seventy feet. The presently accepted estimate is an intermediate figure of fifty-one feet, twice the wingspread of the largest previously known flying reptile, and about five times that of today's California condor. Pterosaurs evidently were excellent gliders, much like vultures, but how a creature of such tremendous size and weight was able to launch itself into the air may always remain a mystery.

High in the Chisos, the Lost Mine Trail begins at Panther Pass, just beneath the massive, lava-rock summit of Casa Grande. As the sun's first golden glow sidelights this imposing peak, the cool mountain air is scented with sweet fragrances of Mexican piñon (*Pinus cembroides*) and alligator and drooping junipers. Black-crested titmice and tiny bushtits chatter as they hunt for seeds, and noisy flocks of Mexican jays fly back and forth on the mountainsides.

The trail climbs through the oak-pine woodland, reaching a narrow ridge of lava rock—an igneous dike nicknamed the Chinese Wall. From there the view sweeps across to the lava-capped South Rim, down into the wide basin of Juniper Canyon, and through the canyon's mouth to the desert expanse beyond. Zigzagging up and up, the trail comes at last to the summit of Lost Mine Ridge, in a final stretch that meanders through a tranquil grove of pines and onto a bold, rocky headland. From this precarious place, the vastness and grandeur of the Big Bend country are overwhelming. Great splintered peaks, deep mountain canyons, and the encircling desert reach far into the hazy distance of Mexico.

Secluded in the shadowed depths below Lost Mine Ridge is Pine Canyon. We hiked into it one October day when wreaths of cloud hung about the peaks above. After climbing from the upper edge of the sotol-dotted desert grassland and into the narrowing canyon, we followed the trail into a cool woodland of Emory and Chisos red oaks, piñons, junipers, a scattering of tall ponderosa pines, and a few picturesque Texas madrones (*Arbutus texana*). Members of the heather family, the madrones are readily identified by their shiny evergreen leaves, clusters of bright red fruit, and thin reddish-brown bark that peels, exposing the smooth, whitish inner bark on its gracefully spreading branches.

We found masses of flaming red flowers on a shrub called mountain sage, while beneath a grove of bigtooth maples, at the cliff-encircled canyon's end, were a few late-blooming yellow flowers of the delicate longspur columbine (*Aquilegia longissima*).

The Basin, a beautiful, grassy expanse completely ringed by bold rocky promontories, nestles in the heart of the Chisos. Trails branch from it. One leads down the slopes to The Window, where a stream dashes through a narrow slot in the cliffs, disappears over a brink of water-polished rock, and plunges seventy-five feet toward the desert below.

The climactic hike in the park is on the trail that switchbacks four and a half miles up and out of The Basin, winding through meadows and sunny woodlands of oaks, junipers, and pines, coming, at last, to the top of Emory Peak. The last few feet are a tricky scramble up splintered boulders. Suddenly there is nothing—or everything, depending on your point of view! You are more than a vertical mile above the Rio Grande, and the whole world of Big Bend drops away from these few square feet of barren rock.

From this dizzying spot you can see the long fault escarpment along the east side of Mesa de Anguila, gashed by Santa Elena Canyon, nearly twenty miles to the west; and the Sierra del Carmen, more than twenty-five miles to the east. Stretches of the Rio Grande are faintly visible toward the south. Clustered around the foreground of the 360-degree panorama is a jumble of Chisos peaks surrounded by the endless expanse of desert. We were caught in a thunderstorm at the top of Emory one April afternoon as cumulus clouds began building quickly. By the time we were back in the meadows of The Basin, dramatic black clouds were bearing down on the peaks, thunder was rumbling overhead, and cool, refreshing rain was beginning to fall.

There has been a lot of human history here—of early Indian tribes and later marauding bands of Apaches, and of overgrazing by sheep and cattle in the late nineteenth and early twentieth centuries. So remote and rugged was the Big Bend that its deep Rio Grande gorges had not even been explored until 1899, when Dr. Robert T. Hill, leading a geological survey expedition, floated three hundred and fifty miles from Presidio to Langtry, Texas.

Here, too, are the sites of Glenn Spring, one of the region's earliest American settlements; the ruins of the old Mariscal mine, where cinnabar was discovered; the one-time health spa and trading post of Hot Springs; and Castolon, a U.S. Army post which stood guard against Pancho Villa's raiders from 1919 to 1925.

Across the river from Big Bend are two little Mexican frontier villages. Boquillas, near the base of Sierra del Carmen, began as a lead, silver, and zinc mining center; Santa Elena, across from Castolon, is mostly an agricultural community. Santa Elena seems ages removed from modern times. The wide, dusty main street, the store, the school, the many little flat-roofed adobe homes, and the church with its tiny bell tower all blend with the earth in the shadow of the imposing Mesa de Anguila. Life here is poor by some standards, but as people come and go—a man on horseback, women busy with their daily chores, others tending crops, and a couple of little boys going from house to house showing off their morning's catch of fish from the river—the relaxed pace of life seems an integral part of the mood of the desert, a mood that reflects the baking heat of long summers and the simplicity of the vast and lonely landscape.

The winds of time have been blowing for ages in the Tularosa Basin of southern New Mexico. They have picked up grains of selenite gypsum crystals from the dry lake bed of the Ice Age's Lake Lucero, and spread out a magnificent, glistening landscape of pure white sand dunes.

The dunes are not always as white as snow. Just before sunrise the rolling sea of sand is a soft purplish-blue. As the sun slowly creeps from behind the high, rugged wall of the Sacramento Mountains, a pinkish-orange glow warms the rounded crests of the highest dunes. The sun mounts higher, and slanting light creates contrasting dark shadows of the crescent-shaped dunes, stretching across the intervening flats, in intricate wind-ripple patterns and among a million tiny footprints left by the myriad forms of nocturnal animal life. Only in the blinding glare of midday are the dunes a shadowless white expanse that stretches nearly thirty miles in length and nearly ten miles across.

The dunes of White Sands lie close to the northern limit of the Chihuahuan Desert. Vast shrubby areas of creosote bush, mesquite, and saltbush surround the dunes. At their outer margins tall-stalked soaptree yucca (*Yucca elata*) grows. In the late afternoon the narrow, sword-like basal leaves and tall flower or fruit stalks of the yucca cast long shadows across the sand.

In the interior of the constantly shifting dunes, on interdunal flats, scattered clumps of olive-green leafless ephedra dot the sands, along with four-wing saltbush, rubber rabbit brush, and various beautiful grasses and wildflowers. Springtime brings contrasting touches of pink, purple, and yellow; in autumn, rabbit brush and snakeweed provide bright patches of golden orange.

One wonders how any plants manage to survive in such a hostile environment. Some develop extensive root systems that reach down to the soil beneath the dunes. A few struggle to survive the onslaught of shifting sands by lengthening their stems from ten to twenty feet to keep themselves from being buried. Such is the remarkable adaptability of the yucca, skunkbush sumac, and occasional small cottonwood tree.

Animals, too, have developed special ways of coping with the environment. Most of the desert-and-dunes creatures are active at night—both to avoid the intense heat and light of the sun and to find greater protection from enemies under the cover of darkness.

A number of dune-dwelling mammals, reptiles, amphibians, and insects have evolved lighter protective coloration than members of their species inhabiting other places. Gophers and mice, spade-foot toads and lizards, scorpions and beetles are all lighter than they normally are in other environments.

The earless lizard can turn so white that it is completely camouflaged when it is lying motionless on the sand. A usually buff-colored species of pocket mouse is found in three different color phases: white fur of those in the White Sands area, reddish of those living in the nearby desert, and very dark brown of those dwelling in the black contorted expanse of the forty-four-mile-long lava flow of the Carrizozo Malpais extending north from the White Sands.

Sitting on top of a high dune, feeling the cool, soft sand on bare feet, watching the last light of the sun gild the sands encourages contemplation of how this landscape was created. The dunes and desert mountains had their beginning between two hundred and two hundred and eighty million years ago when a long arm of the sea reached far inland. The seawater evaporated along the shallows of bays and lagoons, leaving behind calcium-containing gypsum. Over aeons these deposits became five-to-six-hundred-foot-thick beds of selenite.

Under a somewhat deeper sea, deposits of lime, silt, and clay were subsequently deposited and compacted into huge thicknesses of limestone and shale. Finally, as the sea drained away some seventy million years ago, the region began slowly to lift—a movement related to the building of the Rocky Mountains. About ten million years ago a great chunk of land began faulting and dropping slowly downward, until the hundred-mile-long, thirty-mile-wide Tularosa Basin was formed, bounded on the east and west by escarpments of the ancient layered limestone, shale, and gypsum—the Sacramento and San Andres mountain ranges.

As there is no outlet from this graben, or basin, eroded mountain sediments, notably gypsum, have been carried for millions of years to the lowest point, Lake Lucero, setting the stage for the creation of the White Sands.

One wonders what mysterious acts of their gods the early people of this region may have attributed to such a landscape. Apparently the earliest people here were nomadic hunters—Folsom man, who chipped projectile points with which to kill a large species of bison and other now-extinct species of wildlife. That was between ten and twelve thousand years ago. Between six and seven hundred years ago a more sedentary agricultural people occupied the region, growing crops of corn, beans, and squash.

Marks left by past inhabitants are to be seen fifty miles northeast of the White Sands, near the base of Sierra Blanca Peak, where the Three Rivers petroglyphs are scattered along the crest of a low ridge in the creosote-bush desert. Artists of the Jornada branch of the Mogollon Indian culture of southwestern New Mexico chipped and carved stylized motifs in the jumble of black basaltic boulders. Masked faces, mountain sheep, birds, lizards, and strange geometric designs are still clearly discernible, in spite of between six hundred and one thousand years of exposure to the weather.

As you stand on the ridgetop at Three Rivers, with a March wind whipping across your face, the world takes on a very different perspective. Time falls away and the eye roams far and wide over the surrounding desert. Nearby, snow-capped Sierra Blanca rises majestically, while in the foreground lava-capped foothill mesas jut from the desert floor. The wind carries its own strange silence and raises a cloud of white dust from the distant White Sands.

Borders and sheets of silver ice glisten on ponds and marshy places in the early-morning sun. Frost crystals sparkle like jeweled embroidery on long, curled cattail leaves, while their brown, sausage-shaped catkins are backlighted in a halo of fuzzy seeds. Dense stands of tall, plumy phragmites flutter in a light breeze, against the background of distant snow-covered mountains.

On a beautiful, crisp December day flocks of quacking mallards, shovelers, pintails, and other ducks crowd patches of open water, some taking off, circling, and splashing down again. A pair of elegant white whistling swans waddle across a slippery expanse of ice. Beside the dike road a half dozen Canada geese sit quietly in a patch of ice-encrusted grasses. Farther on, a mile-long flock of red-winged and yellow-headed blackbirds weave and sway over the fields and marshlands—thousands of them passing overhead as if on some great pilgrimage along the Rio Grande.

Near the northern end of the Chihuahuan Desert the marshes of Bosque del Apache provide one of the most important wintering areas for migratory birds crossing the American Southwest. About a quarter of the area is river bottomland, a patchwork of pastures, fields of grain, diked ponds, canals, marshes, and extensive bosques of ancient, spreading cottonwood trees. Years ago these groves provided sheltered camping places for bands of Apache Indians roaming back and forth across southern New Mexico.

Bordering the expanse of floodplain are gently sloping, arroyo-cut desert foothills and mesas that are covered mostly with the olive-green creosote bush. Beyond, to the west, rise the pine-clad San Mateo Mountains.

Wintering birdlife fills Bosque del Apache from late November through January or early February. Visits in all seasons can be rewarding (the two hundred and eighty species of birds that have been recorded there include many nesting songbirds), and in late fall and early winter thousands of greater sandhill cranes (*Grus canadensis*) and snow geese (*Chen hyperborea*) crowd into the refuge. The Fish and Wildlife Service's estimates indicate that on this day 7800 cranes and 13,000 geese have arrived.

An unmistakable sound can be heard: the honking chorus of the deep, rolling, guttural calls of the sandhill cranes. As we drive beyond a hedgerow of willows, tamarisks, and cottonwoods, there they are—several thousand of the slender, stately, four-foot-tall birds. Their soft gray and rust-brown-flecked plumage blends with the surrounding fields, and there are literally acres of them, their long necks and heads poking up out of the rows of tall, dry corn stalks.

Cranes leap into the air together and float back to earth on broad wings. Amid a din of excited calls, small flocks take off and gracefully flap and glide to new places nearby, while other groups come winging in to join the crowd.

A few cranes along the hedgerow are curious about us and come cautiously closer, all the while reaching down with their long beaks for bits of grain. As we look through binoculars, the brilliant red forehead patches of the adult birds stand out like beacons.

Wintering sandhills have long attracted attention along the Rio Grande. In 1540 the first Spanish explorers of New Mexico, led by Francisco Vásquez de Coronado, reported seeing "a very large number of cranes." Three centuries later one of the earliest naturalists to explore the desert Southwest, Lieutenant James W. Abert, made an autumn trip along the Rio Grande and wrote that the flocks of sandhill cranes "kept up a great whooping."

Subsequent slaughter and habitat destruction greatly reduced the total crane population, until the crane was considered an endangered species. In 1939 the Bosque del Apache National Wildlife Refuge was established, largely to protect and improve the major wintering area of these birds. Since then this area has played a significant role in restoring their numbers, and today Bosque attracts the largest winter concentration of greater sandhills in North America—in some years numbering ten thousand cranes.

These Rocky Mountain flocks migrate in spring to marshy breeding areas in southwestern Montana and adjacent Idaho and Wyoming. In early autumn they congregate at a refuge in southeastern Idaho. In October the birds make an amazing nonstop flight, climbing to 14,000 feet as they cross some of the high peaks of the Colorado Rockies. They pause for rest and food at refuges in the upper Rio

Grande watershed in southern Colorado's San Luis Valley. Then, flock by flock, they continue southward, flying high above the Rio Grande. Often they are barely visible in the sky; yet their croaking calls carry for miles. All through November and early December the cranes arrive at Bosque del Apache and at other wintering areas in southern New Mexico and northern Mexico. By early March most or all of them have begun their long journey northward again.

The sound of the sandhills still fills the air long after we leave the fields and continue along the fifteen-mile refuge tour route that goes by a stretch of the bosques. The magnificent autumn gold has faded from the cottonwoods. The dry, brown leaves have not yet fallen, and a light breeze rattles them like paper. The road swings around the north end of the refuge, passing several large pastures that have been mowed to provide resting and feeding areas for great numbers of snow geese.

We are just beginning to speculate about where all the geese can be when, far off to the southwest, a huge billowing cloud of white specks erupts into the air, against the backdrop of the mountains. We faintly hear the steady, high-pitched murmur of cries. It is so even-toned that it sounds like an enormous swarm of buzzing bees.

Louder and closer the cloud comes in an undulating, flickering mass, with separate lines of birds strung out like long white streamers. The thousands upon thousands of geese head directly for the pastures beside us, circle, slow, and land, covering the ground like a vast snowbank. Grabbing camera, telephoto lens, and tripod, I begin inching toward them and come to within just a few yards of the closest edge of the concentration. They are preoccupied with feeding on the grain and shoots of grass and seem totally unconcerned.

Suddenly, as if on cue, a great part of the congregation rises en masse. Hundreds of their whirling, black-tipped white wings fill the camera frame at a time, accompanied by the deafening sound of their cries. Standing among the milling birds, I remember that snow geese fly four thousand miles or more from the desert to spend the summer raising their young in the far north arctic tundra of Canada, Alaska, and even Siberia.

The final thrill of the mid-December day comes as the warm late-afternoon sunlight slants across Bosque, accenting the variety of neutral gray and brown tones of the trees and grasses, and casting long dark shadows behind the mountains. A few brief calls of geese come from a different direction, and out of the southern sky appears a rapidly flying V of snow geese, then another and more. For fully three-quarters of an hour, wave upon wave of curving lines and V's race overhead. Each in turn circles in the golden light, slows, and joins the multitude already spread across the fields.

Two mule deer snort their alarm and speed across a meadow. Soon coyotes will begin howling to each other, and night creatures—the bobcats, raccoons, skunks, and great horned owls—will be out hunting along the bosques.

The Chiricahua Mountains rise abruptly, like a great green island, from a surrounding sea of desert and desert grasslands in the southeastern corner of Arizona. Covered with forests and slashed by rocky canyons, they provide a range of five life zones, from Lower Sonoran to Hudsonian, with an amazing variety of flora and fauna, much of it representative of neighboring Mexico.

Photographs hardly prepare one for the incredible landscapes on the western side of the range. Nor is there any real hint of what lies ahead, as you follow the paved road from Willcox across the wide-open desert grasslands of Sulphur Springs Valley and enter the broad mouth of Bonita Canyon.

The canyon narrows and divides, and an oak woodland provides the setting for a campground. Abruptly the scene changes. Tier upon tier of buff-colored columns, pinnacles, and other great monolithic shapes cover the steep canyon slopes. Where the rock has been vertically fractured and weathered, enormous close-ranked organ-pipe formations rise high above shaded groves of gray-green Arizona cypress trees.

Several miles farther on, at Massai Point, the road ends high up in the mountains. The panorama sweeps across an endless array of rock figures covering the ridges and deeply cut canyons. In the far distance, two thousand feet below, the flat, brown expanse of valley stretches off toward the Dragoon Mountains, forty miles away.

Trails lead down from Massai, delightfully looping for miles through the Wonderland of Rocks. On a perfect late-winter morning the air is cool and the bright sun is warm, even hot, in sheltered places. The way winds down through a fragrant open forest of Mexican piñons and oaks, and follows an intimate side canyon where there are groves of alligator junipers, cypresses, and a few tall Chihuahua pines (*Pinus leiophylla*). Several tall rock columns rise out of the forest, looking like an ancient Roman ruin.

Rounding a bend, the trail emerges into wider and deeper Rhyolite Canyon and is surrounded by ranks of columnar rock formations, some weathered into angular shapes, almost as if carved by man.

The warmth of the sun bakes into the canyon, bringing out the sweet aromas of juniper and other plant life. Now and then a handsome Mexican Yarrow's spiny lizard, with a white-bordered black collar, dashes across the trail or whisks into a crevice. Even at this season a few clumps of yellow, red, and blue wildflowers are in bloom.

A branch of the trail turns into Echo Canyon. The cool shade provides ideal conditions for the graceful cypresses. Some are a hundred feet tall, with straight trunks of two or three feet in diameter. At a darkly wooded place called Echo Park we rest for a while, listening to the gentle whispering of the wind in the pines and the chattering of little bridled titmice, bushtits, and ruby-crowned kinglets.

The climax comes as the trail switchbacks out of the narrow canyon. Sheer rock walls, great fractured boulders, and flat-topped rocks stair-step up the mountainsides. Tall Apache pines (*Pinus engelmannii*), their foot-long needles shining in the slanting sun, rise from the canyon bottom against shadowed cliffs. We wind on, exploring intriguing passageways and ledges, and peer through narrow slots in the rocks that frame vignettes of scenery. Low-growing piñons, junipers, and clumps of red-barked pointleaf manzanita give the feeling of a carefully tended Oriental garden.

On a hot April day we hike along a five-hour loop trail through the spectacular, unbelievable Heart of Rocks. It is noon by the time we reach our destination, and we picnic atop a flat boulder. The hundreds upon hundreds of formations rising all around give us the eerie feeling that they are a huge audience of giant spectators while we, the actors, are performing for their silent enjoyment.

Nearby we find the largest of the balanced rocks—an immense chunk—its many tons perched precariously on a tiny pedestal. Even a human figure standing at its massive base inadequately conveys a sense of its true size.

The geologic history of this area dates back to between ten and twenty-five million years ago, when the land was jolted, burned, and smothered by a long series of extremely violent volcanic eruptions. Huge clouds of white-hot ash, sand, and gas poured from the earth. As each successive outburst settled and cooled, the ash and sand gradually welded together, forming hard layers of rock, a rhyolite tuff. Cooling also caused contraction and fracturing of the rock. As pressures within the earth slowly uplifted these mountains, exposing the volcanic material, erosion and weathering took advantage of the fractures and cracks, gradually producing the weird, rocky landscape.

Over on the eastern side of the Chiricahuas, in the deep, sheer-walled gash of Cave Creek Canyon which strikes southwest into the heart of the range, an incredible variety of plant and animal life attracts birders, scholars, and scientists from all over the world. At the American Museum of Natural History's Southwestern Research Station every conceivable aspect of the natural environment—from raptors, lizards, snakes, and ants, to grasses and the microscopic hairs on the abdomen of tarantulas—is studied.

From the broad expanse of grazing land in San Simon Valley, along the Arizona–New Mexico border, an alluvial slope, or bajada, sweeps up to the foothills of the Chiricahuas. In great stretches of this valley its bajadas are sparsely grown with grasses, desert wildflowers, and low-growing desert perennials, such as snakeweed, creosote bush, mesquite, white thorn, small-leaved sumac, soaptree yucca, ocotillo, and tarbush, the last specifically indicating that the Chihuahuan Desert extends barely this far to the northwest.

Another common plant is an *Ephedra* called Mexican-tea. This relative of the pines is a yellowish-olive-green shrub with long-jointed, upright stems, leaves reduced to mere tiny scales, and small yellowish flowers that bloom from cones. Indians and Mexicans have long derived a tea drink from this and other species of *Ephedra* of the deserts.

During a Christmas bird count one year, we visited this open creosote-bush country. Moisture from a light rainfall the night before brought out the pungent desert fragrances. At sunrise as we checked out a cattle pond for ducks, the musical yapping of a coyote drifted across the land, and two of these handsome animals came loping into view along a low ridge a quarter of a mile away. In a grove of trees near a rancher's windmill, we saw two or three dozen mountain bluebirds—brilliant light blue in the morning sun. As we explored the desert all day, and added new birds to a count that eventually totaled more than thirty species, we watched patterns of clouds pass overhead, casting dark shadows, changing and re-coloring the broad valley and distant mountains.

Where the tiny community of Portal nestles along the sycamore-bordered creek, the entrance to Cave Creek Canyon is a wide amphitheater, framed on one side by a high, ocotillo-covered foothill ridge of uptilted limestone strata, and on the other by the pink and brown cliffs and towering ramparts of Silver Peak and Cathedral Rock. This first view into Cave Creek is one of the most impressive canyon landscapes anywhere in the desert Southwest.

Scenery alone would make this place outstanding, but at the transition zone between the upper edge of the desert and the lower edge of the riparian and mountain woodlands, there is so much more.

Bands of peccaries feed on the fibrous, succulent leaves of agaves and cacti, take midday siestas on the shaded banks of an irrigation ditch, and crisscross the mesquite thickets on their "pig paths." They sometimes savagely snarl and bark at each other and lock jaws in vicious fights. At a bend of a trail, where it dips across a hidden dry wash, we once came upon a couple of peccaries with a tiny reddish young one. It was so sudden that for a brief moment or two, while the peccaries stood there and snorted, we were not sure whether we would have to climb a nearby thorny mesquite tree or they would dash away. Peccaries can run or bound off in great leaps with amazing speed. But they are very shy, their eyesight is poor, and they are dangerous when cornered—especially with their young.

In all our time here we have seen very few snakes. Yet it is in the vicinity of Portal that more than eighty per cent of the United States' medical supply of antisnake venom is collected.

I have had the companionship of a beautiful, nonpoisonous, four-foot-long greenish Sonora whipsnake, which slips into a crack in the outside wall beneath the window next to my desk. He travels like liquid lightning, zipping over shrubs and along the vine-covered side of the house.

One evening we saw a tiny fifteen-inch-long banded red, yellow, and black Arizona coral snake hurrying along the front patio. Very distressed at being noticed, he, cobra-like, raised his black-nosed head and hissed aggressively until he slipped into a narrow crack. The coral snake's venom is highly dangerous, but its mouth is so small that the snake would normally find it difficult to bite a person.

There are a number of species of rattlesnakes in this vicinity, some nocturnal and all dangerously venomous. Each occupies a particular type of habitat. The bold, hostile gray or light brown western diamondback rattler and the most venomous greenish Mojave rattler normally live in the open, brushy desert of San Simon Valley. The yellow, gray, or olive black-tailed rattler dwells in the lower woodlands, often near rocky outcrops and stream courses. The rare banded rock rattler lives in upper canyon rockslides, and the gray or brownish-gray twin-spotted rattler (an endangered species) dwells in the rocky talus slopes at higher elevations of the mountains. The twin-spotted rattler is usually relatively mild-mannered, and his rattle sounds like the soft buzz of a cicada.

The Sonora gopher snake which, at first glance, looks like a rattler with bold, dark blotches down his back, is frequently seen during the daytime. He is easy to distinguish because he has no rattles, and his head is small and slender, unlike the broad, spade-shaped head of a rattlesnake.

During part of our stay in Portal, the area suffered one of the worst droughts in the Southwest's history. The forests and desert were tinder-dry, and during the summer a single day's lightning storm started a score of fires in the high country. Whitetail deer came to browse in all the gardens. Waking early in the morning, we would see from three to ten deer in the yard, munching contentedly on rose bushes and any other lush green thing in sight. At the slightest alarm their tails flipped up and, with grace and beauty, the deer would leap the high stone wall and stand on the other side, hoping we would not realize they were still there, waiting to return.

We have seen tiny faces and the delicate paws of skunks as they peered through the windowpane of the patio door, and a mother raccoon instructing her four tiny young ones where the best handouts were on the front porch.

The coati (*Nasua narica*), which barely ranges into the Southwest from Mexico, is closely related to the raccoon. Coatis have long, slender snouts and long furry, faintly ringed brown-and-black tails. Playful and curious, they poke into everything and eat almost anything. We have frequently seen them up the wooded south fork of the canyon, where they climb trees and steep rocky slopes, using their tails to balance themselves. Late one afternoon we saw seven impish young coatis scampering around the trickle of water in the creek and clambering over boulders, curving tails held high.

Occasionally we have even seen a beautiful Apache fox squirrel (*Sciurus apache*) in the wooded canyon. In the United States, this golden-brown animal is found only in the Chircahua Mountains.

Of all the birdlife in and around Portal the roadrunner (*Geococcyx californianus*) has been the most fun. When the neighboring ornithologists went East one summer, my wife volunteered to feed the two wild roadrunners, nicknamed Rhoda, which they were studying, and which they did not want to lose track of during their absence. The birds had hatched a young one a few weeks earlier, and now all three would come running when Pam called "Rhoda!" at the top of her lungs. They quickly caught on to her routine, and when she occasionally failed to appear on time, one of them would run up the road to our place, stand on the front steps and *"brrruuuutt"* until she appeared. Then the impatient bird would run down the road at her heels, chattering and hurrying her on. Roadrunners are friendly, comical, and intelligent, and seem to remember you. For all the remaining months of our stay in Portal, "our" Rhodas continued to talk to us and to roost at night in a cypress tree by the front gate.

Spring brings a tremendous influx of other birdlife. There are the softly cooing white-winged and mourning doves, melodious yellow-and-black Scott's orioles, black-headed grosbeaks, summer and western tanagers, and cardinals. Less musical but strikingly beautiful are the orange-and-black hooded and Bullock's orioles. We have seen as many as fifty or sixty of these orioles at one time, flocking around bird feeders.

Scores of hummingbirds fly in from the tropics: tiny black-chinned, rufous, and broad-tailed; the large, striking Rivoli's and blue-throated; and once a rare calliope. Incessantly they zip and whirl and hold themselves suspended in mid-air around the nectar feeders. The sun catches their flashing iridescent markings of green, blue, red, orange, and purple. Only Ramsey Canyon, seventy miles southwest of Portal, near the Mexican border in the Huachuca Mountains, boasts more kinds of hummers than Portal.

Warblers, those colorful and musical little birds that flood northward in spring through the forests of the eastern United States, are attracted to the Chiricahuas in surprising numbers too. Audubon warblers and red-white-and-black painted redstarts are year-round residents, while in April others come in from Mexico: Wilson's, Lucy's, Townsend's, Grace's, Macgillivray's, olive, black-throated gray, and the unmistakably stunning red-faced warbler.

The "rattle-rattle" cactus wrens, whose deep, round nests are all over the place in the prickly pear and cholla cacti, are local residents. Curve-billed thrashers also frequently build nests in spine-protected places. One summer we watched and photographed a pair of these birds as they raised two broods of young in a huge cholla. They laid beautiful little deep-turquoise-blue eggs and seemed able to raise only two young ones at a time. If more eggs were laid, they were simply not allowed to hatch.

As the young birds grew and seemed ready to fly, the parent thrashers tempted them to a perch in a nearby cactus or tree, luring them with food. When the young birds were really able to fly away, a parent then sat in the nest and edged each baby out. Several days after leaving the nest, the young birds were searching for food on their own.

Three species of quail inhabit the Portal area. The "cotton-top" scaled quail flock together out in San Simon Valley; the recently renamed Montezuma, or fool's quail, live secretively in the lower woodlands; and the Gambel's quail, with forward-curving topknot, are abundant in the desert-woodland transition. It is the Gambel's that we have watched most often, as pairs or flocks scurry through thickets or march single file along our stone wall. They usually manage to keep their broods of tiny, fuzzy young ones well hidden, but once in a while a cluster of little quail scoots across an open area, close behind mother and accompanied by lots of clucking sounds.

Early in the morning and again in the late afternoon a dozen or more of the male quail perch in mesquites or on tall old agave stalks, all across the canyon, repeating their two-or-three-note calls again and again. There is always a maverick; one bird ends his call with a high-pitched squeak that sounds as though he had laryngitis.

Cave Creek Canyon shelters a number of raptors: golden eagles, red-tailed, ferruginous, Cooper's, and sharp-shinned hawks. At night, great-horned owls and screech owls hoot softly.

Of all the birds of Cave Creek Canyon, the most exciting is the coppery-tailed trogon (*Trogon elegans*). This colorful, tropical, fruit-eating bird arrives in May, to breed in just a few places north of the Mexican border—among them the south fork of Cave Creek Canyon and Madera Canyon in the

Santa Rita Mountains south of Tucson. The male's striking plumage is a glossy dark green, with bright rosy-red breast and a long black-tipped tail.

Up the South Fork, a delightful trail winds for miles along the level, gradually narrowing canyon bottom, passing through sunny groves of Arizona white and silverleaf oaks, Arizona madrones, cypresses, sycamores, little clumps of bigtooth maples, and the tall Chihuahua and Apache pines.

It is an intimate world along the dashing creek. Massive orange and pink cliffs, covered with expanses of yellowish-green lichen, rise high above the trail. Caves of all sizes and shapes are dotted along the canyon walls, but most are inaccessible or reached only if one scrambles up the steep talus slopes.

In spring large patches of yellow and red columbine come into bloom along the stream banks, and there are tiny purple violets and monkey flowers here and there. In July, after thunderstorms have brought the first soaking rains, the woods have the sweet odor of dampness. It is then that the mountain yucca (*Yucca schottii*) comes into blossom, its great stalks of creamy-white bell-shaped flowers scattered all through the woodlands.

A dirt road crosses over the Chiricahuas, between Cave Creek Canyon and the national monument. At Onion Saddle a road branches to the south, leading to Rustler Park, where fragrant, stately ponderosa pines, Douglas firs, and Mexican white pines grow in the sheltered mountain basin.

We have been up at Rustler when gale-force winds of springtime were slamming into the crests of the mountains and roaring through the ridgetop trees. In winter snow covers the meadows and weights down the pine and fir branches, and the air is fresh and invigorating. In early summer rain clouds settle onto the mountain summits like a Maine coast fog, and the flute-like songs of hermit thrushes drift through the misty forest.

Toward the south, the Crest Trail climbs high into the Chiricahua Wilderness, where summits top-out at more than 9700 feet. Engelmann spruces, white firs, and little groves of aspens are reminders of the Colorado Rockies. Wisps of fragrant beard lichen grow thickly on branches and tree trunks. The musical trills of juncos, the raucous calls of the crested Steller's jays, the twitterings of pygmy nuthatches, and the soft, raspy calls of Mexican chickadees are heard. Meadows are filled with tall purple larkspurs, blue irises and lupines. Only the small clumps of hedgehog cactus nestled on rocky outcrops, and the distant views of Sulphur Springs and San Simon valleys remind you that this "northern" world is closely surrounded by the vastness of the desert.

Symbols of the Desert

The Arizona-Sonoran Desert

In the Sonoran Desert, just outside of Tucson, Arizona, thousands of strange cacti, from forty to fifty feet high, dot the bajadas and lower mountain slopes for miles. Although it is found only in parts of the Arizona–Sonoran Desert (barely overlapping into southeastern California and extending southward into Mexico), the saguaro (*Cereus giganteus* or *Carnegiea gigantea*) has become the popular symbol of deserts in general.

These giants begin as vulnerable little seedlings that are eaten by such creatures as pack rats, mice, and weevil larvae, and may be killed by the direct rays of the baking summer sun. To survive the sun's onslaught, they must start their first few years of growth in the shade of a host tree, shrub, or rock crevice, until the stem becomes covered with a thick, waxy layer that insulates the cactus and reduces the loss of moisture.

Saguaros take an incredibly long time to grow and mature. After two years they are a mere quarter of an inch high. After ten years they measure only from four to six inches. First flowers do not appear until thirty or forty years, when the cactus may be ten feet tall. Not until sometime after seventy-five years of age does the single-stemmed column finally begin putting out its first armlike branches. When you see a saguaro with five or ten upraised branches (occasional veterans have as many as fifty or sixty), you can be sure it is somewhere between a hundred and two hundred years old.

Considering the size of these great cacti, and the fierce winds that sometimes whip across the desert, you would assume that they have sturdy, deep taproots. But the intricate root system lies only a few inches beneath the ground surface and extends outward from thirty to sixty feet in all directions. Such a wide reach enables the plant to absorb as much moisture as possible during the infrequent summer and winter rainstorms. When saguaros soak up great amounts of rain, their pulpy water-storage tissue, surrounding the interior woody skeleton, expands like the pleats of an accordian. The spine-covered vertical ridges of the main stem and branches become "fattened," and a large cactus may weigh eight or ten tons. Nearly ninety per cent of this weight is water—a ton of which may be the moisture absorbed during just a single rainfall.

In May and early June, as the sun's heat begins to bake the desert, prominent waxy white flowers burst forth in clusters at the tips of branches and the main stem. A few at a time magically open in the evening and remain out until the following afternoon, attracting white-winged doves, longnose bats, insects, and Gila woodpeckers to their nectar.

In late June and July the saguaro fruits mature, splitting open to expose a mass of reddish pulp that is filled with black seeds. A great variety of birds feed on the fruits and seeds. Those that are knocked off and fall to the ground are eaten by ground squirrels, pack rats, coyotes, and harvester ants. In some parts of the desert Papago Indians still follow their ancient custom of harvesting saguaro fruits; they use a long stick, called a kuibut, to gather them. They eat some of the pulpy fruit raw; the rest is dried in the sun. The juice is boiled down for syrup and jam.

Most saguaros are pockmarked with round holes drilled by Gila woodpeckers and gilded flickers. These birds hammer away, searching for insect larvae or hollowing out nest sites in which to raise their young. Their abandoned holes sometimes provide daytime sleeping and nesting quarters for screech owls, pygmy owls, or the tiny, sparrow-sized elf owls whose soft calls drift across the desert at night.

Widely spaced among the saguaros are the softly spreading foothill or yellow paloverdes (*Cercidium microphyllum*). These graceful trees and the similar blue paloverde (*C. floridum*) that grows along arroyos are covered in spring with magnificent masses of tiny yellow pea-like blossoms that perfume the desert air, attracting colonies of humming bees. For a short time the paloverde puts out tiny leaves. As soon as the dry, baking heat of summer sets in, the leaves are shed, to reduce the loss of plant moisture by transpiration. The green chlorophyll in the bark of the trunk and branches, for which the species is named, continues the work of food making.

Other members of the saguaro desert landscape are mesquites, catclaw acacias, ocotillos, and creosote bush. The leathery, evergreen-leaved jojoba or goatnut (*Simmondsia chinensis*) bears seeds that were once eaten by Indians of southern Arizona and southern California, or were boiled to make a coffee-like drink. Desert marigolds and deep apricot-flowered globe mallows bloom profusely in spring, along with the delicate pink-and-red-tasseled fairydusters or calliandras, and crimson Parry's penstemons. One of the most profusely blooming shrubs is brittlebush or incienso (*Encelia farinosa*). It has grayish, hairy leaves and small sunflower-like yellow blossoms on long stems, and it is common throughout much of the Sonoran, Colorado, and Mojave deserts.

The Sonoran has more species of cacti than any other desert in the American West. In late spring, summer, and early fall, vast reaches of the desert come alive with their incredible colors. There is the curve-spined, squat-looking barrel cactus, that wears a crown of yellow or vibrant orange blossoms after summer rains in July; the yellow-flowered prickly pear; delicate little fishhook and pincushion cacti; deep magenta or pink Fendler's hedgehog; and a number of the extremely spiny chollas. Teddy-bear cholla is thickly covered with sharply barbed pale yellow spines, while purple or pink-flowered chain-fruit cholla has long, grotesque pendent masses of fruits. Staghorn or buckhorn has spring flowers that vary from plant to plant—from yellow, orange, red, and purple, to brown and green. Desert Christmas cactus has slender joints and yellowish flowers and conspicuous little red fruits that brighten the winter landscape.

After winters of normal or exceptional rainfall, the desert becomes a striking tapestry of wild-flower annuals. These spring ephemerals must have enough rainfall to wash out growth-inhibiting chemicals. The seeds then quickly sprout, put forth a wealth of flowers, produce a new crop of seeds, and die before early summer's heat and drought set in. There are masses of low-growing bright yellow bladder-pods; pale yellow desert dandelions; yellow evening primroses; white tackstems; violet-blue phacelias; yellow-orange fiddle-necks; delicate blue lupines; purplish-blue larkspurs; reddish-purple owl clovers; and many, many more.

Immediately east of the urban sprawl of Tucson is the Rincon Mountains unit of Saguaro National Monument. In the saguaro–paloverde desert on a calm spring day you will hear the gentle, persistent cooing of doves, cheerful songs of bright red cardinals and cardinal-like pyrrhuloxias, calls and clucking of Gambel's quail, high-pitched notes of tiny verdins, short whistles of the black crested phainopeplas, "rattle-rattle-rattle" of the cactus wrens, piercing "whit-whits" of curve-billed thrashers, and tinkling trills of black-throated sparrows.

Although most desert mammals avoid the heat of the day, occasionally a lone coyote, several mule deer, or bands of peccaries cross the trails. Jackrabbits suddenly leap from hiding places and go tearing off across the desert. A little desert cottontail will run off a few paces, then sit stock-still, thinking you can no longer see him.

Most obvious of the eight-legged arthropods is the large, hairy, but virtually harmless tarantula. There are several species of scorpions with long, arching tails that end with a poisonous stinger. While all scorpions can inflict a painful sting, only one, a two-inch-long, slender-tailed, straw-colored species (*Centruroides sculpturatus*), injects venom that can be fatal to man, particularly to young children.

In the sloping rocky foothills of Tanque Verde Ridge saguaros, prickly pears, hedgehog and fishhook cacti, teddy-bear and other chollas are nestled on every ledge, nook, and cranny. Ocotillos, jojobas, paloverdes, and many desert wildflowers grow all around the outcroppings of ancient banded rock known as Catalina gneiss. This attractive metamorphic formation was created by aeons of tremendous pressures and heat deep within the earth, and uplifted some twenty to thirty million years ago. Rich in mica, quartz, feldspar, and hornblende, the rock sparkles like a pile of jewels in the bright sunshine.

Higher along the ridge, panoramas open out toward the long, canyon-gashed mountain ranges. From this point you get a wonderful feeling of the rocky, arid desert, sweetly perfumed with faint spicy aromas of desert plant life.

From the 2500 to 4000 feet elevations of the Sonoran Desert, the Tanque Verde Ridge trail climbs up and up into the high country of the Rincon Mountains, passing through five other major biotic communities.

From the desert and desert grassland the trail leads on through open oak and pine woodlands, up to the Canadian-like stands of Douglas fir, white fir, and aspen, atop the cool, damp north slopes of Rincon Peak and Mica Mountain.

West of the city, on the far side of the Tucson Mountains, the saguaros are generally younger than many of the giants east of the city, but the landscape is far more densely forested. In late afternoon shadows emphasize the columnar pattern of the hundreds upon hundreds of green cactus stems. A breeze now and then hisses softly through the millions of spines.

As the last rays of the sun glance across Avra Valley, the rocky cliffs and summits of the mountains are flooded with rich orange light. Quickly the sun drops behind distant purple mountain ranges, and the black profiles of the cacti are etched like sentinels against the bright evening sky. Desert sunsets are extremely beautiful, especially when there are a few streamers of cloud that the sun sets ablaze with the most dazzling shades of orange and red. In the dry, clear desert atmosphere the sky is often aglow for an hour before the light fades away.

Later, under a bright canopy of stars and the delicate sliver of a crescent moon, a coyote, wandering along a nearby arroyo, suddenly breaks forth with wild musical howling and yapping. His excited jumble of variously pitched notes sounds like a chorus rather than a solo. For long minutes his singing continues. Then, far across the desert, another echoes the first. The night begins.

Only an hour's drive from the sea, there is a sweep of desert that for us combines just the right feeling of remoteness with a complete blending of typical and unusual hot-desert plant life, and a perfect starkness of austere, volcanic mountains. Its beauty is framed by the tall forms of organ-pipe cactus that here ranges briefly northward across the Mexican border into southwestern Arizona.

Dominating the eastern end of Organ Pipe Cactus National Monument is the magnificently raw, reddish-chocolate-brown mass of the Ajo Mountains. A dusty twenty-one-mile road climbs eastward through saguaro country that is carpeted in spring with reddish-purple owl clovers, yellow brittlebush, blue lupines, and yellow-and-orange Mexican poppies (*Eschscholtzia mexicana*). As the serrated mountain escarpment draws closer, its crumpled rocky canyons, ridges, and ramparts become more clearly defined.

And then the Ajos suddenly tower high above you, looking as if they had been squeezed up out of the earth by some gigantic cataclysmic event. And so they were. Geologists have calculated that there were tremendous outpourings of molten lava during the Tertiary era, between ten and forty million years ago. This material, deep within the earth, cooled and hardened into great thicknesses of andesite (tuff), breccia, and basaltic lava flows. More recently this basin-and-range region was subjected to tremendous pressures that caused gradual uplifting of long blocks of the land. The Ajos are among the many resulting ranges.

Because of the sparse rainfall—roughly eight inches a year—and because the mountains rise to only 4800 feet, they are almost devoid of vegetation, unlike the higher, forested ranges, such as the Chiricahuas, in southeastern Arizona.

The name Ajo comes from the small but elegant white ajo or desert lily (*Hesperocallis undulata*) that blooms fragrantly in March and April. Early Spanish explorers named the plant "ajo" because its large edible bulbous root was garlic-like.

The drive swings southward along the base of the towering escarpment, winding through foothills and lower canyons. There are spectacular views at every turn, framed by saguaros, ocotillos, chollas, and imposing candelabra-stemmed organ-pipe cacti (*Cereus* or *Lemaireocereus thurberi*).

Intolerant of frost, the organ pipes range only a short way into the United States, scattered mostly about the south-facing slopes of Sonoyta Valley, that sweeps north from Mexico. The largest of the organ-pipe cacti have from twenty to thirty ribbed, columnar stems rising impressively fifteen or twenty feet from the ground. In May, when this area is beginning to feel the sun's baking heat, the organ pipes put out white flowers that are lightly tinged with pinkish lavender. But to see this show of elegance, you must be up early, for they bloom at night and fade right after sunrise.

Where the road swings close to the imposing Ajos, a two-mile trail leads up through boulder-strewn Estes Canyon and climbs a ridge affording organ-pipe-framed views far across the desert to distant mountains. The end of the hike overlooks Bull Pasture, a hidden, cliff-encircled place of grass, yuccas, agaves, and ocotillos.

Back on the loop drive, the road descends into Sonoyta Valley, affording a view far into Mexico. Along this stretch, where teddy-bear chollas grow densely, we spotted our first desert rattlesnake. He was stretched out almost full-length by the side of the road, his light tan color and faint diamond-shaped markings along his back blending well with the desert gravel. He gently rattled the end of his tail—just a reminder that we should keep our distance.

On an April morning, when the temperature was still cool, we started out along the fifty-one-mile Puerto Blanco Drive. The slanting light added dramatic shadows and glowed through tall golden grass that mixed with creosote bush across the broad desert plains.

We stopped to photograph the landscape, and suddenly a slight shuffling noise on the ground nearby caught our attention. At first we suspected a snake, but there beneath a creosote bush lay an eighteen-inch-long orange-and-black Gila monster (*Heloderma suspectum*), the only poisonous lizard in the United States. Actually sluggish and nonaggressive, Gila monsters rarely bite unless provoked. They can snap quickly and will persistently chew on their enemy or prey until the venom is forced into the wound from glands in the lower jaw. We watched this one for a while, as he eyed us with what appeared to be calm suspicion.

Our next stop was at a cheerful place called Dripping Springs, on the side of a rocky hill. From a cliff above, a trickle of water splashes into a small pool, from which the barest flow of water drips on down until it disappears into the ground. A wreath of lush greenery grows all around the tiny oasis. Scores of hummingbirds zip in and out, gathering nectar from tall-stalked red penstemons and other flowers, and doves flock in for water.

From the springs the dusty road strikes on across the desert between the Puerto Blanco and Growler mountains, with Kino Peak rising prominently beyond. In dry washes, paloverdes, mesquite, and desert ironwood trees—all members of the pea family—provide narrow bands of riparian woodland.

The ironwood (*Olneya tesota*), which grows between twenty and thirty feet tall, thrives in the hottest areas of southwestern Arizona and southeastern California. It is intolerant of frost. Contrasting with the smooth, bluish-green bark of the paloverde, ironwood trunks and branches are rough, gray, and almost stringy. True to its name, the wood is extremely hard and heavy, quickly dulling a saw or ax. In May, the trees burst forth in a profusion of wisteria-like purplish-and-white flowers that are faintly fragrant. Except during periods of extreme drought, the ironwood is covered with small gray-green pinnate leaves. As I once discovered while crawling under one of these spreading trees to photograph a flowering cactus, the branches are armed with extremely sharp thorns.

Where Puerto Blanco Drive reaches the Mexican border and begins its eastward return, there is another place of permanent water—a delightful spring-fed pond called Quitobaquito. It is bordered by old cottonwoods, their lush green contrasting with the surrounding desert. Bulrushes and sedges grow thickly around the edges of open water. Coots swim in and out of the dense reeds, while grebes constantly dive beneath the surface for food. A kingfisher perches on a dead cottonwood branch, diving into the water to catch a fish now and then. Phainopeplas, Gila woodpeckers, doves, warblers, cardinals, phoebes, and the dazzling vermilion flycatcher fill this beatiful oasis with color and song. Nearly two hundred kinds of birds have been recorded here—an incredible total for so small a place.

The final highlight along this route is the senita cactus (*Cereus* or *Lophocereus schottii*). Although its many columnar stems look much like the organ pipe, it is nicknamed "the old one" because the long spines, thickly covering the upper ends of the clustered stems, look like gray hair. The stems differ further from the organ pipe by growing only ten or twelve feet tall and by having fewer and more pronounced ribs. Small pale pink flowers open their petals at night during May and June. There are few senitas, for this Mexican species ranges just into the southern edge of the monument.

Surprisingly, a southwest wind at times brings the sweet, damp odor of the ocean to the desert. The arid landscape seems a million miles from any expanse of water. Yet, cross the border at Lukeville and drive for sixty miles, and you are suddenly in a totally different world. At the road's end is the little Mexican town of Puerto Peñasco, with fishing boats—some in various stages of construction—along the shore. A white sandy beach curves to the north in a broad crescent along the bright blue expanse of the Gulf of California. It is a particularly beautiful spot where one can see and feel the incredible contrast between the desert and the sea.

The Colorful Inferno

The Colorado Desert

Ethereal smoke trees, sculptured badlands, forests of ocotillo, oases of fan palms, stocky elephant trees, sheer-walled canyons, sunburnt mountains, and shifting earthquake faults make the Anza-Borrego Desert a place of fantasy. Much of the region lies within the nation's largest state park.

This is hot country, horrendously hot in summer, for it is part of southern California's low Colorado Desert, with elevations down to and below sea level. This region of the Salton Basin becomes a baking inferno of crushing, dry heat, with daytime temperatures commonly reaching 115 to 120 degrees or more in the shade. From late spring through mid-autumn it is mostly a place to avoid or to dash across under the cooler cover of darkness. Only in late autumn, winter, and early spring does the thermometer drop low enough to be thoroughly inviting, and at times it is alive with the color of blossoming desert flowers.

The most dramatic approach is from the west, over the high Peninsular Ranges. This great wall of mountains, where oaks, pines, and junipers grow at higher elevations, extends on southward as the backbone of Mexico's Baja California, and it effectively blocks off nearly all the moisture and rainfall from the Pacific Ocean. Annual rainfall averages from barely five inches down to a trace in some parts of the park. The resulting contrast between the ranching, farming, and chaparrel country that extends up to the crest of the mountains on the west, and the parched, pale brown tones of the desert immediately to the east is absolute and awesome.

A highway over the mountains, between Warner Springs and Borrego Springs, provides a spectacular introduction. One moment you are driving through a green brushy land; then the whole world falls away, dropping most of a vertical mile to the desert expanse that is rimmed by barren yet majestically carved mountain ranges.

In mid-April the steep rocky slopes along this switchbacking road are ablaze with the vivid colors of cactus flowers—masses of flaming pink of the beavertail prickly pear (*Opuntia basilaris*), and glowing crimson-magenta of the strawberry hedgehog (*Echinocereus engelmannii*).

On the sloping desert bajadas and vast flats far below, late winter and spring flowers create a fantastic tapestry of colors that transforms the face of the land—if the winter has brought moisture sufficient to trigger the floral exuberance. Sandy areas become carpeted with pink sand verbena and white desert primrose. Vibrant shades of yellow, orange, red, blue, and purple flowers spread across dry washes and bajadas. The spiny clumps of tall ocotillo put out tiny leaves and terminal clusters of scarlet-orange flowers.

A few miles east of the resort community of Borrego Springs lies the water-eroded landscape of the Borrego badlands. A narrow sandy road, turning south from the paved Borrego–Salton Seaway, follows a dry wash and ends at the impressive promontory of Font's Point. In the late-afternoon sun the undulating, rippled maze of barren forms is etched in a repetitive pattern of light and shadow, a dramatic panorama that can hardly be imagined under the flat, glaring light of midday.

Far beyond the badlands and the vastnesses of the desert where creosote bush and white bur sage (*Franseria dumosa*) grow sparsely, purple-hued mountains rise along the horizon. To the north, evening sunlight glances along the crumpled ridges, spurs, and crests of the massive Santa Rosa Mountains.

Miles to the south of the badlands, beyond a lonely desert crossroads settlement called Ocotillo Wells, a paved road ends at the dry wash of Fish Creek. This arroyo emerges from a meandering, sheer-walled gorge that cuts through Split Mountain. Sand, gravel, boulders, and battered debris litter the gorge, evidence that terrifying flash floods from summer cloudbursts occasionally sweep down like roaring tidal waves.

Early morning is peaceful and cool. The slanting sun casts dark shadows along the light, buff-colored cliffs, which in some places rise more than five hundred feet. At one part of the cliff base tremendous forces within the earth have somehow twisted the horizontal layers of sandstone into an upthrust dome-shaped formation, the swirled rock of an anticlinal fold.

A few smoke trees (*Dalea spinosa*) are scattered here and there in the stream channel, looking much like puffs of campfire smoke rising from the sand. Most of the older trees rise from a battered base of splintered branches and lodged debris. The almost misty appearance of their unsymmetrical upper branches is accentuated by slanting rays of early morning or evening sun and seems even more ghostly under the light of a full moon.

This shrubby tree, which ranges from a few feet to fifteen or twenty feet in height, is found exclusively in sandy washes and arroyos throughout the Colorado Desert of California, parts of southwestern Arizona, and southward into Mexico. Its mazes of silvery gray-green twigs are generously armed with long spines, but in early summer it is transformed by a magical profusion of fragrant bright bluish-violet flowers.

To reproduce, the smoke tree is totally dependent upon heavy summer cloudbursts. Its dormant seeds must be carried along by a sufficient deluge of water to scrape off the outer covering and leach out acids that prevent premature germination. The churning flood of mud-laden water must carry the seed far enough, but not too far, downstream. If insufficient water flows, the seed—like those of so many other desert plants—will simply wait.

Near Anza–Borrego's Split Mountain canyon another incredible desert tree can be found. A short distance north of the canyon a rough, rocky track branches westward for a mile, and from there a trail continues another mile and a half up the gently sloping, boulder-covered bajada valley. The walk itself is delightful—red chuparosa and yellow brittlebush are out in January, and there are many of the pinkish, southward-tilting compass barrel cacti.

The first elephant tree (*Bursera microphylla*) is rather battered from all the handling and twig-breaking by the curious. But a little way beyond, a magnificent example stands amid a jumble of gray granite boulders. The stout and stocky trunk divides close to the ground into a number of angular, arm-like branches that sharply taper to a pattern of slender twigs. Trunk and branches are covered with papery pinkish-golden bark, and twigs bear minute, dark-green, pinnate leaves. Most of the other widely scattered elephant trees in the vicinity (some five hundred have been counted) are only four or five feet high. This one rises eight or ten feet, with a horizontal spread greater than its height.

It is an exotic, majestic-looking tree—something you'd expect would be extremely rare in the United States but common in a tropical region. Botanists believe elephant trees are slow-growing, and there is no doubt that they look like weathered veterans that have struggled for a long time against the harsh elements of the desert. There is apparently no way to tell just how old they are, for they do not put on growth rings as oak or pine do. The wood is rather cork-like and is very lightweight. Elephant trees are found only in this part of the Anza–Borrego, in some of the arid mountains of southwestern Arizona, and southward into Mexico.

In mid-April the temperature here can be uncomfortably hot by midday, reaching ninety degrees or more in the shade, so we set out early one warm, lazy morning to explore Borrego Palm Canyon. Along the dry washes we found indigobush (*Dalea fremontii*), covered with tiny, sweet-scented, deep blue-violet blossoms. From a buckhorn cholla cactus, boasting inconspicuous pale greenish-yellow flowers, a cactus wren sang his scratchy song. Lizards darted across the trail or lay sunning themselves.

The winding canyon gradually narrows between its steeply rising, rocky slopes at the base of the San Ysidro Mountains. Ironwood, mesquite, catclaw acacia, and desert willow border the dry stream course. Although it has willow-like leaves, *Chilopsis linearis* is not a true willow but is related to the catalpa. Its angular-branching shape, with foot-long hanging seedpods, is commonly seen along arroyos from southern California to west Texas. It is particularly striking when adorned with inch-long lavender-white orchid-like flowers.

Nearly a mile and a half from our start, we suddenly spotted a patch of surprisingly lush green ahead—a few California fan palms (*Washingtonia filifera*). Farther on, into the main grove of palms, deep shade offered refreshing, damp coolness from the already baking, dehydrating heat of the sun.

Some of the palms are short and stocky, while others have slender trunks rising forty feet high. The old dead leaves of fan palms do not fall off. Unless fire has burned them, they hang down beneath the head of green fans, closely covering the trunks like brown shirts that rustle and rattle with the slightest breeze.

In spring vivid orange-and-black hooded orioles fly back and forth from palm to palm where their nests of young are hidden. The canyon resounds with the richly melodious songs of the yellow-and-black Scott's orioles. Tiny iridescent-green hummingbirds loop and zip through the air in amazing courtship flights—almost too fast for the eye to follow. Somewhere far up the barren rocky slope a canyon wren solos a cascading trill of notes.

At night desert oases like this attract all kinds of wildlife—among them mule deer, an occasional mountain lion, bobcats, coyotes, foxes, ring-tailed cats, raccoons. The desert bighorn sheep dwells in the Santa Rosas, San Ysidros, and other rugged mountainous areas of the park, and can occasionally be seen at such a stream at night. (The Anza–Borrego takes its name in part from the bighorns; "borrego" is the Spanish word for the bighorn yearling or lamb.)

Near the upper end of the palm oasis, where the clear stream squeezes between giant boulders, a modest waterfall drops a few feet into a pool below. Here in the otherwise parched desert, beneath the canopy of bright green palm fronds, the sight and sound of gently falling water cast a magic spell, heightening realization of just how valuable water is to all life. This palm grove, stream, and wildlife are but a microcosm of the whole earth. In a hostile environment especially, you come closer to understanding just how delicately balanced the world's life-support systems are.

These fan palms and others dotted around the Colorado Desert are evidently tropical remnants of a greater abundance and wider distribution, dating from a far wetter climate of the Pleistocene epoch. Pockets of palms like this always indicate the availability of water—sometimes heavily alkaline water, but water nevertheless. If there is not a stream above ground, then there is water just beneath the surface, flowing down from the mountains or being forced up toward the surface by the earthquake faults that lace and periodically jolt this region.

Approximately ninety known palm groves are scattered around the Colorado Desert, many hidden far from main highways and jeep trails, in remote spots difficult to reach. Some are tucked away elsewhere in the Anza–Borrego, in pockets concealed in various canyons around the flanks of the Santa Rosa Mountains, along the eastern escarpment of towering Mount San Jacinto, across Coachella Valley at Thousand Palms, along the Indio Hills, and hidden away in the eroded Mecca Hills.

The fan palm is almost entirely restricted to the Colorado Desert and Baja California, except for a couple of palm oases to the north, at the southern edge of the Mojave Desert, and several isolated canyons in the extremely rugged Kofa Mountains in the Sonoran Desert of southwestern Arizona. The largest of the Kofa groves contains about fifty trees that appear to cascade down a steep, narrow cleft, high in the massive, reddish volcanic andesite cliff.

Six miles south of the affluent glow of Palm Springs, in the Agua Caliente Indian Reservation, is the largest and most famous of all the many groves. The view across the glistening top of the hundreds of trees along the floor of Palm Canyon is magnificent. Many of the majestic trees rise fifty or sixty feet. In places they form dense, darkly shaded stands. The trail leads southward up the canyon, following a stream that is also bordered by sycamores, willows, alders, and tamarisk. On the arid slopes above are creosote bush, mesquite, catclaw acacia, and barrel cactus. Seven miles up the canyon the trail reaches a refreshing waterfall.

Towering ten thousand feet above the desert at Palm Springs is one of America's sheerest mountain escarpments—the bold east face of Mount San Jacinto. This gigantic mountain, reaching spectacularly from palms to pines, and Mount San Gorgonio to the north, form a natural gateway between the Colorado Desert and the Los Angeles basin and Pacific Ocean to the west. San Gorgonio Pass, between the twin giants, is often an immense wind tunnel, with phenomenal volumes of air rushing fiercely between the mountains and stirring up blinding sandstorms in the desert.

Desert of Contrasts

The Mojave Desert

Twenty-five miles east of the cultivated date groves of the Coachella Valley at Indio, California, a paved road strikes north from the highway, beginning a spectacular and unique climb from the Colorado Desert to the Mojave Desert. For miles the road climbs higher and higher into the mountains at the eastern end of the great Transverse Ranges that extend into the desert all the way from the Pacific Ocean.

Straddling the great mountain barrier between the two great deserts is a nature reserve of rare Joshua trees, a place of magnificent landscapes and striking contrasts. It is a fitting introduction to the extremes of the Mojave Desert where pressures within the earth have produced tremendous changes in altitude and distinctly different life zones.

Ironwoods, paloverdes, and smoke trees grow along the dry washes of the southern edge of the Joshua Tree National Monument. From the delightful oasis of Cottonwood Spring, a four-mile trail winds up and down eroded mud hills and arroyos, and descends into a steep gorge to a hidden spot called Lost Palms, where the tropical green foliage is a temptation to linger.

Higher in the mountains lies the broad treeless bowl called Pinto Basin, rimmed by barren desert mountains. In the middle of the creosote-bush plain is a dense stand of ocotillos, indicating that this valley is part of the low desert. Higher up the gently sloping bajada grows one of the most impressive "forests" of teddy-bear cholla (*Opuntia bigelovii*) to be found anywhere. In late afternoon these densely spined cacti, five or six feet tall, become dramatically backlighted, their silvery-yellow spines glowing against the distant shadowed mountains.

Joints of this branching cactus dislodge so easily that it is sometimes called jumping cholla. Once you are ensnared, a painfully barbed piece lodges itself first in one place and then another; the furry-looking teddy bear has a friendly reluctance to let go!

The road climbs higher. Just above three thousand feet the landscape suddenly changes and you enter the Mojave Desert. Gigantic outcroppings of rounded buff-colored rocks rise out of the land. At a placed called White Tank a trail leads into the jumble of granite-like quartz monzonite boulders. At the end of the climb a small natural arch frames the view from the commanding heights.

It is believed that these extremely picturesque islands of rocks began some 150 million years ago when hot molten volcanic magma deep within the earth intruded into older overlying rock, and very slowly cooled and crystallized. The overlying material has since eroded away, exposing the monzonite, which in turn has weathered into the endlessly fascinating shapes we see today.

Scattered around the rocky outcroppings are many of the weirdly beautiful Joshua trees. Across some of the high valleys these yuccas (*Yucca brevifolia*) form vast open-grown forests. Queen Valley's flat expanse is dotted with them, while Lost Horse Valley is even more densely forested. At Cap Rock a short nature trail winds through a higher area where Joshuas merge with junipers and piñons. A steep two-mile climb to the top of nearby Ryan Mountain provides an impressive view across Queen, Lost Horse, Hidden, and Pleasant valleys.

A few miles to the south, on the crest of the Little San Bernardino Mountains, is Salton View, one of the most spectacular panoramas in the western deserts. A mile below sprawls Coachella Valley, with the twin peaks of San Jacinto and San Gorgonio to the west, the shining surface of the Salton Sea thirty miles to the south, while Signal Peak, its summit suspended above the haze, rises ninety miles away in Mexico.

In April Joshua Tree monument is stunningly beautiful. If there has been enough winter precipitation, the great yuccas rise from glowing carpets of yellow and pink wildflowers, and many of the Joshua hold out massive panicles of tightly clustered greenish-creamy-white blossoms at the ends of their branches. Unlike those of other yuccas, the Joshua flowers do not open widely.

At Jumbo Rocks beautifully sculptured monzonite formations and a few scattered Joshuas set the stage for spring's splashes of yellow, blue, pink, and purple flowers, climaxed by clumps of the most brilliant scarlet paintbrush. In winter a light mantle of rare snow may briefly dust the Joshua branches making them look like fluffy white brooms.

The Joshua tree, one of the tallest members of the lily family, is the largest of the fifteen or so varieties of yuccas in the United States. In the 1880s Mormon pioneers saw in its outflung, angular branches a symbolic representation of the Biblical account of Moses' servant and successor as he beckoned with outstretched arms to the Israelites to follow him from the desert to the Promised Land of Canaan.

Although it is not possible to determine exactly the age of Joshua trees, it is estimated that the largest may be at least five hundred years old. They are generally between fifteen and thirty feet tall (occasionally forty or more), with crowns up to twenty feet across.

Young Joshuas do not begin branching from their single stalk until after they produce their first panicle of flowers. And so they continue over the years: a new branch grows out at an angle from the base of each faded flowerhead, creating the characteristic twisted arm-like appearance.

Joshua trees can be pollinated only by *Pronuba synthetica*—a modest little gray moth. At dusk the female moth flutters from flower to flower, gathering a sufficient amount of pollen. She then lays her eggs in the ovary of a blossom, also depositing some of the pollen to assure fertilization of the flower. The Joshua tree returns the favor by providing a few of its seeds as food for newly hatching *Pronuba* larvae in a perfect example of symbiosis.

The tiny desert night lizard *Xantusia vigilis* also relies largely upon the Joshua, finding shelter and termites among the overlapping masses of dry leaves that cover the trunk and fallen branches. Pack rats, Scott's orioles, screech owls, bluebirds, flycatchers, wrens, woodpeckers, and many other creatures of the desert also depend upon Joshua trees for nest sites or as sources of insects.

Many kinds of lizards inhabit the monument; the largest is the eighteen-inch-long chuckwalla (*Sauromalus obesus*), best known for its extraordinary ability to scurry into a rock crevice and quickly inflate itself to half again its normal size so that enemies cannot pry it loose. The finely beaded skin of chuckwallas varies in color from black to grayish-brown, with irregular patches of orange or reddish-brown. Chuckwallas are vegetarians, and unlike the Gila monster of the Sonoran Desert, are non-poisonous. However, if they are provoked or cornered, their bite can be painful.

As the key plant indicator of the Mojave Desert, the Joshua tree grows in scattered areas in northwestern Arizona, extreme southwestern Utah, southern Nevada, and elsewhere in California. Joshua trees are also found near Cajon Pass along the northern foothills of the San Gabriel Mountains, and farther west, near Lancaster in Antelope Valley. This valley, at the far western end of the Mojave Desert, is also famous for its displays of acres upon acres of brilliant orange California poppies, yellow coreopsis and goldfields, pale yellow desert dandelions, blue lupines, bluish-purple phacelias, reddish-purple owl clovers, and many other wildflowers.

Heavy winter rains in 1973 produced a rare and extravagant April floral show on the desert with carpets of coreopsis (*Coreopsis bigelovii*) to the east of Lancaster, and poppies (*Eschscholtzia glyptosperma*) to the west. On the rolling hills called Antelope Buttes and Fairmont Butte, the orange poppies were most spectacular. Much of this area is being saved as a new state park.

Most of the land farther east, filled with yellow coreopsis, is unprotected except for a few all-too-small wildflower and wildlife sanctuaries, and its remaining wildness is steadily being wiped out. Where earlier we photographed vast sweeps of flowers, real estate speculators had already scarred the desert with preliminary developments for tract housing projects. Paved roads, complete with curbing, signposts, and fire hydrants, were laid out in typical grid pattern. Such is the fate of many areas of the desert.

We are up early one morning, winding in darkness through a rocky maze called the Alabama Hills, looking for a spot from which to see and photograph the high drama of sunrise on the tremendous eastern escarpment of the Sierra Nevada.

As the first hint of dawn faintly brightens the sky eastward over the silhouetted Inyo Mountains, we set up cameras at a promontory far up among the rock formations. The mysterious hooting of an owl drifts up from a shadowy ravine.

The light in the east softly illuminates the Sierra's jagged peaks, which thrust upward more than two miles above America's deepest valley. The cool air is fragrant and invigorating. Minutes pass in silence. As we wait, a rosy glow catches the narrow top of Mount Whitney. Soon the color spotlights other peaks all along the range—Mount Williamson to the north, the whole series of serrated pinnacles of the Whitney group, and the massive, angular summit of Lone Pine Peak straight ahead. In seconds the entire snowy crest is brilliantly gilded with vibrant reddish-gold.

The tide of color flows down and down the sheer mountainsides, accentuating the distant details of snow, rocks, and trees. Imperceptibly, the rich color changes to orange, yellow, and finally to white. When the sunlight reaches the base of the range, only the desert floor of Owens Valley before us remains in the shadow of the foreground hills.

Later in the April morning we explore a scenic gravel road that branches west off the highway north of Lone Pine and winds through a rocky landscape where bold granite outcroppings frame the mountains. Brilliant clumps of vivid scarlet paintbrush dot the desert, and an iridescent green hummingbird darts from flower to flower.

Only the gentlest breeze stirs the desert plants. We perch on a mound of huge boulders absorbing all the incredible beauty around us, the sun's warmth, and the spicy desert fragrances. How did the earth's immense forces create so grand a scene?

Somewhere between 80 and 150 million years ago, roughly coinciding with the age of the great dinosaurs, the basic substance of today's Sierra Nevada and Inyo Mountains was formed. At very long, irregular intervals molten magma pushed from deep within the earth toward the surface. Slowly this cooled, forming a crystalline structure that hardened into granitic rock. During unimaginably long aeons great thicknesses of strata, overlying the batholiths of granite, eroded away.

From ten to eleven million years ago the major uplift and westward tilting of the Sierra Nevada began to occur. A mere one and a half to two million years ago, massive faulting, along the eastern escarpment of the Sierra, was accompanied by an accelerated downdropping of Owens Valley many thousands of feet, almost to its present level.

The Alabama Hills, extending for about ten miles along the floor of the valley in a line parallel to the mountains, are part of the same ancient granite, but because of the uplifting of the mountains and down-faulting of the valley, they are two miles below their counterparts on the mountain crests. While the granite of the high peaks has been splintered and shaped by snow and ice, the Alabama Hills have been more gently sculptured by wind and rain into rounded forms. The jumble of boulders among these hills has for years been the scene of wild chases, ambushes, and mock gun battles staged for movie and television Westerns.

The tremendous faulting and uplifting forces within the earth that created the spectacular mountain-bordered valley are still active today. Although at a somewhat slower rate, perhaps, than in times past, these forces are nonetheless measurably increasing the height of the four-hundred-mile-long Sierra Nevada, shifting the gigantic land masses and now and then sending tremors throughout the deepest valley. A major fault zone lies right at the eastern base of the Alabama Hills and runs for more than a hundred miles along much of Owens Valley.

The greatest earthquake ever recorded in the deepest valley occurred in the span of a few terrifying seconds in the pre-dawn hours of March 26, 1872. Lone Pine was hardest hit. As the quake rippled through the ground, nearly a score of people lost their lives, many others were injured, and most of the town's adobe buildings were demolished. Land lying along the fault zone dropped as much as twenty-three feet, creating a cliff-like scarp that is still visible. The shock was felt 280 miles to the south in San Diego and 400 miles north at Mount Shasta. The pioneer naturalist–conservationist, John Muir, in the Sierra Nevada's Yosemite Valley at the time, heard tremendous rock falls triggered by the earthquake.

A side trip up into the Sierra escarpment from Owens Valley is an experience in exhilarating contrasts. West of Lone Pine the road climbs from 3700 to 8300 feet, among the tall, fragrant Jeffrey pines and white firs at Whitney Portal. All the way up the steeply switchbacking road, there are breathtaking views back down to the brown expanse of desert and twenty miles across to the rounded summit of the Inyos. Late in the afternoon the Sierra's long, angular black shadows creep far across the valley and up the pinkish slopes of the Inyo range. In September big clumps of rich golden-flowered rabbit brush brighten the roadsides. At the end of the road a trail leads off past a waterfall and begins its steep climb more than ten miles to the flat summit of Mount Whitney. Others climb over the crest of the Sierra, into the wilderness high country.

Driving in late April from Owens Valley into the Sierra escarpment west of the small community of Independence, sixteen miles north of Lone Pine, we found 9000-foot Onion Valley freezing cold, with a wintry wind blowing a gale through battered old red firs. Several feet of snow covered the ground —a scene that gave no hint of summer's lush green meadows where lilies, gentians, orchids, fireweed, and monkshood bloom. Steep slopes of scree sweep up to imposing granite peaks towering far above.

From the dizzying heights of Kearsarge Pass you see not only the deep trough of Owens Valley but far eastward to the desert ranges that border Panamint and Death valleys. Below, the town of Independence is barely visible.

Mary Austin lived in Independence from 1892 to 1903. Inspired by the contrasting worlds of the desert and mountains, she wrote in *The Land of Little Rain*, "Here you have no rain when all the earth cries for it, or quick downpours called cloud-bursts for violence. A land of lost rivers, with little in it to love; yet a land that once visited must be come back to inevitably."

A land of little rain it is. While the western slope of the Sierra Nevada may receive from forty to sixty inches of precipitation annually, just a few miles away as the crow flies, the lower Mojave Desert of Owens Valley receives a mere three-to-ten inches. Just south of Lone Pine, Route 136 strikes out southeastward to connect with Route 190 to Death Valley. Mile by mile, as you draw away from the High Sierra, you can see the land becoming drier and the desert vegetation sparser. It is then easy to understand the term "rain shadow" and see just how the Sierra Nevada blocks and captures for itself nearly all the moisture sweeping eastward with storms off the Pacific Ocean.

From that desert expanse along the highway, the whole enormous sweep of the Sierra is visible. With only low-growing desert shrubs scattered in the foreground, there is nothing to obstruct the spectacular panorama of the range.

In the early morning cotton-puff clouds sometimes quickly gather around the high peaks, casting dark shadows on the slopes below, and the Sierra takes on a mysterious three-dimensional appearance, the softness of the clouds contrasting with the jagged peaks.

Roasting hot days of summer bring huge mountains of billowing thunderheads rising thousands of feet above the Sierra to unleash their fierce barrage of bolts upon the rocky summits. Springtime frequently produces streamlined, lens-shaped clouds that are the sign of powerful waves of wind aloft. Lower winds whip up dust, making the mountains softly recede in haze.

The wild winter storms are incomparable. Like a curtain drawn down to conceal the stage until the next act is ready, clouds completely hide the mountains. Suddenly the morning dawns clear, and the entire range stands out in all its pristine grandeur, the snow line reaching far down toward the floor of Owens Valley. It is a stunning sight!

Northward from Independence, Owens Valley gradually climbs into the higher, cooler sagebrush country of the Great Basin Desert. A few miles along the highway, scattered reddish cinder cones and blackish lava flows lie along the base of the Sierra.

In the vicinity of Big Pine and Bishop, there is clear evidence that Ice Age glaciers once pushed their way down a number of the steep valleys along the Sierra escarpment. Lateral and terminal moraines, the glacial deposits of rocks and gravel, define the outer limits of those tongues of ice.

In this area you may also happen to see a few rare tule elk. This small subspecies was originally native to California's San Joaquin–Sacramento Valley. In 1933, after they were nearly wiped out by thoughtless shooting and habitat destruction, a few of the remaining animals were introduced to Owens Valley. Nearly four hundred of them now live there, and legislation has been introduced to establish a refuge for their protection.

While most of Owens Valley is extremely dry, here and there a stream or irrigation ditch is bordered by groves of giant old cottonwoods, willows, or tall, slender Lombardy poplars. In summer these green oases attract a wide variety of birdlife. Bullock's orioles, black-headed grosbeaks, roadrunners, and valley quail are abundant. The long-tailed black-and-white magpies grace fenceposts along many a mile.

The first beautiful stretch of cottonwoods encountered as you drive north up the valley shades the historic stage-stop settlement of Olancha. Just to the northeast are the rolling Olancha sand dunes and the sprawling expanse of Owens Lake playa. This lake bed is all that remains of a sparkling saline lake that once covered a hundred square miles of the valley—itself a mere remnant of a fifty-mile-long Ice Age lake. It is now difficult to imagine the boats that in the 1870s plied back and forth across this lake, loaded with millions of dollars' worth of silver bullion (mined in the Inyo Mountains and smelted nearby).

When the 233-mile-long Los Angeles Aqueduct was completed in 1933, it diverted most of the water of Owens River and gradually drained the lake. The bitter battle over the valley's water raged for a quarter of a century, and the tale of covert planning, devious legal tactics, broken promises, and dynamited aqueducts is a wild chapter of history. Los Angeles' appropriation of water, however, has in some ways been a blessing in disguise, for it is a major reason that one of America's most spectacular valleys remains so unspoiled and unmarred by the urbanization that has ruined so many other scenic places.

Many deserts are extremely hot and arid, supporting practically no flora or fauna. The Sahara of northern Africa, the Namib of southwestern Africa, the Arabian of Saudi Arabia, and the Atacama along the west coast of South America are among the hottest and driest regions on earth. But Death Valley, California, is *the* hottest desert, with summer maximum temperatures consistently higher than anywhere else in the world.

Averaging a scant one and a half to two inches of precipitation annually, Death Valley is also one of the driest places. Yet on our first night there it rained!

By the next day the rain had ceased and clouds were breaking up and moving eastward. In the storm's wake cool refreshing air was perfumed with the most wonderful earthy fragrance of damp desert. The atmosphere was remarkably clear; the moisture had cleaned the air of the dust that often causes the vast distances to be hazy. This was a perfect time to view Death Valley from the mountain-tops.

The panorama from Dante's View, atop the barren Black Mountains, is grand, awesome, and even a bit terrifying at first. From there the six-thousand-foot dropoff is almost sheer to the bleak salt flats below. Far to the north and south the huge basin extends 130 miles, much of it below sea level.

Across the abyss, twenty-five miles to the west, is the jagged crest of the Panamint Range. The higher elevations around 11,049-foot Telescope Peak were dusted with snow from the night's storm. Far, far beyond the Panamints we could barely see the snowy peaks of the Sierra Nevada—and thus beheld at the same moment both the highest and lowest places in the forty-eight contiguous states.

An icy buffeting wind swept across the summit. As we watched and tried to keep warm, the sun finally began to shine through gaps in the clouds, spotlighting the irregular expanse of salt playa on the valley floor, and the crumpled, eroded slopes of the mountains beyond.

Much of the dark, somber rock of the massive fault scarp that dropped away at our feet consists of gray and black metamorphic formations that are among the oldest material exposed on the face of the earth. Geologists say that the rocks of the Black Mountains date back to or beyond the very earliest forms of life in the world—to the Precambrian era, between one and two billion years ago. They have been squeezed, twisted, uplifted, and subjected to unimaginable heat and pressure stresses within the earth—a process that has transformed them to gneisses, schists, and other ancient rocks.

It takes a while for the eye and mind to adjust to a scene of this magnitude, for there is virtually nothing to give it any human scale or definition. About all you can do is to sit quietly and try to absorb a little feeling of the immensity of both time and space, and of man's smallness in the midst of such grandeur that is Death Valley National Monument.

From the opposite side of the valley, another spectacular view unfolds at the end of a rough road to Aguereberry Point in the Panamints. The valley and the austere Black and Funeral mountains to the east are framed at close hand by tremendous uplifted, tilted ledges and cliffs of banded limestone and dolomite. Thousands of feet of these materials were laid down beneath a shallow, warm sea along the edge of a continent half a billion years ago. Marine fossils of the Paleozoic era have been found in rocks of this age, including simple lime-shelled creatures, corals, and primitive crab-like arthropods called trilobites.

From breathtaking heights such as these, Death Valley looks like the down-dropped fault-block basin, or graben, that it actually is. You can visualize how the great ranges, paralleling the valley floor, have been pushed up during the past million and a half years by incredible pressures within the earth, and how they have been deeply furrowed and serrated by water erosion. Vast quantities of silt, sand, and gravel have been swept down the steep gorges and canyons to the basin below. Geologists estimate that the valley has been filled in with some nine thousand feet of sediment, most of which has eroded down from the mountains. That is nearly as far down to bedrock as the highest mountaintops are above the valley's present surface.

You can also see from here just how the mountains are continuing to erode into the basin. At the mouths of canyons, where streams issue from the base of the ranges, there are great alluvial fans, their leading edges forming rounded tongues of gravel that extend far onto the valley floor. The fans along the base of the Panamint Range are much larger than those opposite, and many of them have coalesced into giant bajadas. The largest of these rise nearly two thousand feet, burying the lower slopes of the mountains. These larger deposits along the western side of the valley indicate that the Panamints have been tilting eastward. This immense earth movement is also tilting the valley in the same direction, as evidenced by the location of the vast salt playa along the eastern edge of the basin.

One may or may not try to understand the complicated intricacies of geology, but the landscapes here do clearly emphasize one general fact that is often less obvious or is obscured by lush vegetation in other regions: that the surface of the land is constantly changing, ever-evolving new landscapes from old ones, through vast periods of time. The very forces that have created "the everlasting hills" are actively at work tearing them down and resculpturing the face of the land. At Golden Canyon, Artist's Palette, Devil's Golf Course, Zabriskie Point, Devil's Cornfield, Mesquite Flat Sand Dunes, Mosaic and Grotto canyons, Badwater, and Ubehebe Crater geological forces have been and are creating scenes of great beauty.

In Golden Canyon a short dirt road leads into the narrow, tortuous gorge of yellow rock, from which a trail winds on to the imposing Red Cathedral. Late-afternoon sun makes the ancient yellow and red lake-bed formations glow with dazzling richness.

Zabriskie Point provides a view across the top of this eroded landscape. The prominent headland of Manly Beacon rises above badlands of beautifully sculptured, uptilted, layered hills of clay that were laid down beneath lakes that existed in a wetter climate. Camels, elephant-like mastodons, and little horses left their tracks imbedded in the soft clay there.

A few miles south along the base of the Black Mountains, a one-way paved road called Artist's Drive winds through a kaleidoscope of colorful hills and washes. The colors of the multihued formations of Artist's Palette—red, orange, yellow, tan, brown, lavender, and green—are caused mostly by the presence of metallic oxides in the volcanic and sedimentary rocks.

A little farther south a spur road and trail lead into a canyon where a massive natural bridge has been carved out by rushing, roaring torrents of water that occasionally sweep down, caused by the "gully-buster" cloudbursts of August.

Badwater, a tiny pond of highly saline water lying almost directly below Dante's View, is fed constantly by a spring that seeps out of the ground along the Death Valley fault—a zone of active earth movement that follows the base of the range for many miles. Although it is saturated with salts, a few forms of animal life dwell in the pool. One is a rare species of snail which biologists say is the only known soft-bodied invertebrate in the world that has adapted itself to such extremely saline conditions.

As the first pink blush of sunrise strikes the snow-covered crest, the Panamint Range is perfectly inverted on the mirrored surface of Badwater. After the sun has dropped behind the Panamints, the desert pool picks up contrasting colors of silhouetted mountains, bright sky, and pink clouds. In the midst of such a vast arid space, a spot of water such as this takes on a magic quality that irresistibly draws the human spirit.

Badwater is but the tiniest remnant of a huge pluvial lake that existed in the valley during the Ice Age. From 25,000 to 50,000 years ago, Lake Manly, at its maximum, was a hundred to a hundred and fifty miles long, and up to six hundred feet deep. Faint traces of the old shorelines are still visible here and there. The last of its increasingly saline waters gradually evaporated between 10,000 and 15,000 years ago, depositing beds of mud and salt that are more than a thousand feet deep. The bed of that ancient lake is today below sea level, with the lowest point in North America just four miles northwest of Badwater at minus 282 feet.

Part of the lake bed is the unearthly landscape called the Devil's Golf Course, where it is almost impossible to walk, for it consists of a vast, whitish expanse of chopped-up-looking salt crystal formations, a foot or two in height. The irregular surface has been and continues to be formed by an upward percolation of ground water that creates salt spires and pinnacles in infinite variety as the water evaporates into the dry desert air.

In the weird landscape of the Devil's Cornfield, about twenty-five miles to the north, blowing sand has caused the native shrub known as arrowweed (*Pluchea sericea*) to grow into massive, tall clumps that look like corn shocks widely spaced on a stretch of the valley floor. Indians once used its stems for arrow shafts.

Beyond the "cornfield" are the magnificent Mesquite Flat Sand Dunes. Their smooth, rolling, graceful waves contrast with the sharp features of the distant mountains. The slanting sun of early morning and late afternoon creates spectacular curving patterns of light and shadow. On a breezy day minute particles of quartz are blown into new rippled patterns, and little clouds of sand skim off the dune crests. On a calm day the muffled silence of the sands conveys a contemplative mood of solitude and simplicity. Walk into the heart of the dunes, where wave upon wave undulate away in all directions. One minute you are in the secret depths of a great trough; the next you are commanding the heights of the rolling sea. In early morning the sands may be crisscrossed with the tracks of coyote, kit fox, mouse, roadrunner, sidewinder, or darkling beetle.

Volcanic eruptions have also left their mark on Death Valley. Ubehebe Crater, at the far northern end of the monument's paved road, is the largest and most impressive cone in a field of smaller ones and is believed to have spewed ash and cinders over the surrounding area some three thousand years ago. Its circular crater measures not quite a half mile across and is close to eight hundred feet deep.

During July and August the valley becomes a blistering torrid inferno where the temperature frequently reaches 120 degrees or more in the shade. Ground readings have been recorded at 190 degrees, and there are many nights when the thermometer never drops below 100 degrees. Accompanying such readings are extremely low amounts of moisture in the air, ranging anywhere from ten down to one per cent humidity.

The valley starts getting hot in late April or early May and stays that way until well through October. In the heat of summer even the wind seems to make matters only worse. The furnace blasts accelerate the process of desiccation and often whip up sandstorms.

Under such hostile conditions, how does anything survive? Looking across the sunburnt expanses of the valley and mountains, you might conclude that in fact nothing much does. Yet, even here there are many species of plants and animals, each adapting in its own special way.

Many flowers are triggered into spring bloom after relatively rainy winters. On one of our visits the land was covered with a display of native wildflowers that old-timers claimed had not been equaled in some four decades. The valley was carpeted with mile upon mile of bright yellow flowers, such as desert sunflower and coreopsis. On higher alluvial slopes and valleys we saw masses of dazzling red paintbrush, exuberant clumps of orange apricot mallow, yellow brittlebush, yellow evening primroses, purple phacelia, white tackstem, and many more. Beavertail prickly pear cactus had burst forth with many shades of vibrant pink blossoms, each more magnificent, it seemed, than the last. In March and April, when the land is alive with such floral splendor, the name "Death Valley" seems totally inappropriate.

Hardy perennials such as desert holly, desert velvet, four-winged saltbush, greasewood, and creosote bush are not only heat- and drought-tolerant but salt-tolerant as well. Desert holly (*Atriplex hymenelytra*) is the most attractive of the halophytes, its little angular, holly-like leaves a pale gray that reflects as much of the sun's heat as possible. Scattered across the rocky alluvial fans and sidelighted by the sun, the leaves are silver against shadowed hillsides.

The Death Valley sage (*Salvia funerea*) is found only in this area. Its spine-tipped leaves are ashy white with a thick covering of hairs, and it blooms with modest light purple flowers.

At a few higher, cooler locations in the monument, the Joshua tree grows. There are not many—a few stands on the west side of the Panamints and on the north side of the Grapevine Mountains to the northeast of the valley.

Higher still in the Panamints and Grapevines are "pygmy forests" of single-needle piñons and junipers. On the highest slopes of Telescope Peak, in complete contrast to the vegetation of the floor of Death Valley, grow a few limber and bristlecone pines. In this tremendous range of life zones, botanists have recorded more than six hundred species of plants and trees.

Night on the desert is one of the most beautiful of all moments in time. Stand and absorb the unique stillness and fragrances of the desert on a warm, calm evening. A canopy of intensely brilliant stars fills the sky overhead. Under a full moon, the dunes and desert floor are flooded with a soft silver glow, and mountains are mysteriously visible in the distance.

Strangers here might not expect to see much wildlife, and they would probably be right. Of the fifty species of mammals that do inhabit this huge area, most burrow away in the ground or under the shade of trees and shrubs during the heat of the day and go out hunting for food only under the cover of darkness. There are coyotes, kit foxes, jackrabbits, cottontails, kangaroo rats, pack rats, antelope ground squirrels, and mice. In the more remote mountain areas one may occasionally see desert bighorn sheep and mule deer. The wild "ee-ah-ing" of a herd of burros may be heard trumpeting from across a mountainside. Descendants of early prospectors' animals, they now roam wild in such places as Wildrose Canyon in the Panamints.

There are lizards and snakes of many kinds. Of the eighteen species of snakes, the only poisonous ones are the silent sidewinder or horned rattlesnake of the sandy lower elevations and the pinkish Panamint speckled rattler. Generally active at night, they are seldom seen during the daytime unless their shaded hiding places are disturbed. The harmless rosy boa, striped whip snake, gopher snake, California lyre snake, red racer, Mojave patch-nosed snake, and king snake mostly inhabit the higher elevations.

None of the seventeen kinds of lizards is poisonous. They range from the little two-to-three-inch-long desert banded gecko and the even smaller desert side-blotched lizard, to the western whiptail, leopard, and collared lizards that are between three and five inches long. There are beautifully banded Panamint alligator lizards, measuring four to six inches, and the western chuckwalla, largest of them all. The prehistoric-looking desert horned lizard would be terrifying if it were not so small.

Nearly three hundred species of birds live in or migrate through Death Valley. Some of the year-round residents are the mockingbird, rock wren, Gambel's quail, roadrunner, burrowing and great horned owls, raven, red-tailed hawk, mallard, and pied-billed grebe. Migratory birds rest at the dune- and saltmarsh-bordered ponds of Saratoga Springs, a serenely beautiful oasis at the extreme southern end of the valley. The rare pupfish (of the genus *Cyprinodon*), only about an inch long and grayish in color, a relic of the Ice Age lakes of the Great Basin and Mojave deserts, also lives here.

Another closely related species of pupfish inhabits Salt Creek, far up the valley near the Devil's Cornfield. Amazingly, these fish have evolved to tolerate water that is at least six times as salty as the ocean and that reaches temperatures hot enough to kill any other kind of fish. A third pupfish lives in the mostly underground aquamarine waters of Devil's Hole, nearby in Nevada.

Biologists believe that there was probably only one species of pupfish during the Pleistocene Ice Age, that it dwelt in the various pluvial lakes and interconnecting rivers. As the region became increasingly arid, populations of pupfish apparently became isolated from one another, and gradually, over thousands of years, evolved slightly different characteristics.

Hundreds of years ago the Indians of Death Valley learned to live with the desert. It is believed that about the middle of the nineteenth century there were perhaps between one hundred and two hundred Panamint (Shoshone) Indians in the Death Valley area. They lived close to springs and migrated seasonally from the valley to the mountains and back again, according to the supplies of food. They gathered pine nuts in the mountains and mesquite beans along the salt flats and hunted bighorn sheep, deer, rabbits, ground squirrels, and lizards. Apparently there was very little that did not provide these frugal people with food, clothing, or shelter. In spite of the extremely demanding task of wresting a living from this difficult land, the women made elegant, beautifully patterned baskets.

The first groups of white emigrants to stumble across Death Valley on the way to seek their fortunes in the California gold fields in 1849 did not know how to cope with the desert. Even though it was the cool month of December, they came perilously close to not getting out of Death Valley alive.

After struggling for weeks across the Great Basin Desert, they came down Furnace Creek Wash, dragged themselves across the flats, and searched in vain for a passable route over the barrier of the Panamint Range. Two of the younger men of the party, who had gone ahead to find help, returned after three weeks with supplies. As they all struggled over the Panamints and out of the great trough, they turned to look back into the place that had nearly claimed their lives, and one of them said, "Good-bye, Death Valley." The name has stuck ever since.

Prospectors and mining booms enlivened the next chapter of valley history, beginning in the 1860s. Panamint City, in Surprise Canyon on the west side of the Panamints, was the valley's first silver boomtown, in the mid-1870s. Today a tall brick chimney and a few crumbling walls at the end of a rough jeep road below the south side of Telescope Peak are about all that remain.

To the north of that great peak, in upper Wildrose Canyon, are other relics of the era—a row of ten giant beehive-shaped stone charcoal kilns. Designed by Swiss engineers, constructed by Chinese laborers, and stoked with piñon wood cut by native Indians, they provided charcoal for the Modoc Mine smelter.

Borax, discovered in the marshy playas of the valley, was the next center of attention, and Death Valley became famous for the twenty-mule teams of 1884 to 1889 that pulled two great ore wagons hitched together with a water trailer—a combined weight of thirty-six tons—on the ten-day journey from Furnace Creek southward over Wingate Pass and on to the railroad depot at Mojave.

Gold was discovered in the hills of Nevada east of Death Valley just after the turn of the century. By 1905 the town of Rhyolite began to boom, ultimately attracting between five thousand and ten thousand people. Its ghostly stone and concrete ruins still stand out starkly against the brown desert hills.

Through the years Death Valley has gradually been made more accessible to visitors. Limited mining of talc, lead, and tungsten is still carried on, and prospecting and the filing of mineral claims are still permitted by law. This unusual situation has created a confusing nightmare in the records of land ownership and in the administration of the area. Desecration of the fragile desert landscapes continues, and construction of mining access roads and mining facilities has put scars on the land that will take centuries to heal.

Since 1971 the mining in the monument has taken on a new and terrifying dimension: large corporations have been moving in with talc and sodium calcium borate strip mining and open-pit mining operations that are wreaking havoc upon the fragile landscape, on a scale that makes the earlier prospectors' diggings look like mere child's play.

At this writing, legislation is pending in Congress that would ban open-pit and strip mining in this monument (and in Organ Pipe Cactus Monument) and would bar the filing of any future mineral claims there. Unless the powerful mining lobby can be defeated, however, it seems likely the bulldozers and other giant earth-gouging machines will continue what *The New York Times* has called "this unwarranted commercial privilege" in an area "dedicated to protecting the natural scenery."

Despite these invasions, there is still great beauty to be seen in Death Valley. November through April is obviously the most enjoyable time to explore Death Valley. If, out of curiosity, you venture into the scorching sink in summer, be sure to go well prepared. In any season the vast distances and starkly eroded land will make an impression you will never forget.

One of the most thrilling experiences in the desert wilds is to come upon a small band of majestic desert bighorn sheep (*Ovis canadensis*) back in a remote canyon or up among the rocky battlements of the mountain ranges. These largest of all desert mammals are symbolic of such wilderness country, for they require solitude far from the disturbances of man and are well adapted to the heat and drought of their environment.

Desert bighorns can live for weeks at a time during the cooler seasons without ever needing to drink water. Even during the desiccating heat of summer, they can go for five or six days, deriving moisture only from the foliage of edible plants. Like most creatures of the desert, they avoid activity during the hottest part of the day by lying in the shade of a rock or tree.

Remarkably agile climbers on steep slopes and precipitous cliffs, bighorns thrive on brinkmanship and travel easily where it is virtually impossible for other animals or man to pursue them. Cushioned hooves help them make spectacular and graceful leaps from rock to rock as they move along the narrowest ledges.

The ultimate drama of the bighorn sheep is the contest between rams during the rutting season. Nonchalant and sleepy-eyed, the two combatants back off from each other. Suddenly, as though released by a giant spring, they lunge at each other, heads and horns lowered. The combined speed of charging rams has been estimated at forty miles an hour—so fast that it is hard for the human eye to follow the action. The resounding impact sounds as though they would surely crack their skulls wide open or at least knock themselves silly, but apparently there are few injuries. They don't even appear dazed as they back off for another tilt, and another.

The desert bighorn belongs to the same species as the Rocky Mountain bighorn sheep, but the desert environment has caused the development of certain basic differences. Smaller and of lighter grayish-buff color, the desert variety has horns that are more outspreading and somewhat thinner than those of their high mountain cousins. Rams are distinguished by massive, coiled horns that measure up to two and a half feet in length along the outer edge of the curl. Ewes have more delicate, shorter horns. Adult sheep stand about three feet high at the shoulder, and generally weigh between 120 and 170 pounds.

The federal government has established a number of refuges primarily to help protect the desert bighorns, and Desert National Wildlife Range in southern Nevada's Mojave Desert is the largest and most important of them.

Barely ten miles north of the limits of sprawling Las Vegas, the utterly wild refuge provides a striking contrast to the neon glitter of Nevada's largest city. As you drive northwest from Las Vegas, one barren-looking mountain range after another looms out of the desert vastness.

Near the southern end of the Sheep Range, a gravel road branches north to the green oasis of Corn Creek Field Station. Corn Creek used to be a stagecoach stop along a nineteenth-century emigrant route to California. Today a few buildings are scattered beneath the cool shade of old cottonwoods, and a reed-bordered pond attracts migrating waterfowl. Just beyond is a large fenced enclosure where a few of the desert bighorns are brought for study and observation. For most visitors, this may be the only opportunity to see these elusive animals.

The refuge was established in 1936 to help save from extermination the then rapidly dwindling numbers of bighorns. Too much shooting and habitat disruption by man had been largely responsible for the decline of the bighorn population in this area to barely three hundred animals. There are now about twelve hundred—the largest single concentration of the species in the western deserts.

The bighorns are most abundant in the Sheep Range, where they live between 3500 and 8500 feet elevations, depending on the season and availability of food. This is where most of the life-giving seeps and springs are located, and where the greatest variety of edible shrubs and flowering plants is found. To enhance the habitat and increase the carrying capacity of the range, most of the watering places have been provided with catchment or "guzzler" devices. The cautious visitor may, with good luck, watch a band of rams and ewes, perhaps accompanied by several lambs, all taking turns for refreshment.

From Corn Creek, the Morman Well Road strikes northeast between the Sheep and Las Vegas ranges, climbing the gently sloping bajada that spreads out from the base of the colorfully banded limestone at the southern end of the Sheep Mountains. Creosote bush and other low-growing desert perennials are sprinkled across the stony surface of the ground, and clumps of long-leaved Mojave yucca (Yucca schidigera) and several kinds of cacti grow here and there. In late afternoon bright sunlight emphasizes the patterns of rock strata of the mountains and brightly backlights the spines of hedgehog, silver cholla, and cottontop cacti.

The route emerges from this lower desert terrain, passing through an open stand of Joshua trees. Higher still is a fragrant forest of junipers and piñons, and finally, at Mormon Pass, an area of tall ponderosa pines. In the subalpine world atop Hayford Peak a few wind-swept pines grow.

Besides the bighorns, the refuge is home for many other species of wildlife, and one of the most intriguing is the desert tortoise (Gopherus agassizii). These prehistoric-looking, heavily armored reptiles live for fifty years or more, grow to at least a foot in length, and range across much of the southwestern desert country. They are larger than the smooth-shelled, colorful box turtle, and their brown, high-domed carapace has a sculptured pattern of growth ridges on each of the shields, or shell sections. Their short, stocky rear legs are almost elephant-like, while the front ones are covered with scales.

To avoid periods of prolonged drought, the desert tortoise digs burrows that often extend ten feet underground and are twenty or thirty feet long. A number may simply wait together in one of these cool dens for months at a time, until rains once again produce a crop of flowering annuals and grasses that provide most of their food. Water stored beneath the upper shell enables them to exist for long periods without drinking, and they also concentrate uric liquids to conserve fluids within the body.

In spite of the existence of laws protecting them, the tortoises are declining throughout much if not most of their range. As increasing numbers of off-road vehicles tear across the open desert, more and more tortoises are being run over—often deliberately. People with firearms all too frequently use the tortoises as living targets. New roads, tract housing projects, and other land developments constantly eradicate areas where tortoises live. Nature reserves therefore become extremely important havens for these animals.

Thirty-five miles northeast of Las Vegas lies the brilliantly colored sandstone landscape of the Valley of Fire. Here, in the midst of the more subdued earth colors of the desert, eroded red sandstone formations loom out of the surrounding terrain. Island after island rises from the desert floor—as though a small part of eastern Utah had been dropped into southern Nevada.

Some 150 million years ago, during the Jurassic period, when dinosaurs lived on earth, this region was even more arid than it is today. Blowing sands were piled into great dunes. These, in time, became compacted into sandstone, which in turn has gradually been uptilted and carved by wind and rain into an endless array of rounded shapes—some stained red by iron oxide, others contrastingly white.

Prehistoric Indians once lived in or near the jumble of rocks. Until about A.D. 1150, Anasazi pueblo dwellers farmed lands in Moapa Valley a few miles to the east. Several outstanding exhibits of their stylized rock art—bighorn sheep, people holding hands, and angular and rounded geometric motifs—were carved into the red walls of Petroglyph Canyon. Near the western end of the park other petroglyphs were carved high on the side of Atlatl Rock, which is named for drawings of a spear-throwing device. Close by is one of the area's most beautiful of many small natural arches.

Sweeping panoramas of jumbled ridges, domes, spires, clefts, and canyons are visible from Rainbow Vista and Fire Canyon Overlook. The rich light of the extremes of the day dramatically accentuates the fiery red color of the rock and casts cool black shadows. Beyond the main masses of sandstone there are smaller outcroppings of red rock that dot the open expanses of desert.

Spring wildflowers also brighten the Valley of Fire: clumps of the delicate orange desert mallows; bright yellow marigolds, brittlebush, and catclaw acacia; white desert chicory and trumpet-shaped datura; lavender mariposa lilies; and bright pink beavertail prickly pear cactus.

Under a calm, starry sky at the Valley of Fire one night, we saw our first "moon bow." Misty and ethereal, a wide, delicate arc of white light lit up the western horizon for a long time, and we fell asleep wondering where it came from and what created it.

Adjoining the Valley of Fire to the east is a huge reserve that encompasses Lake Mead, Lake Mojave, and some of the country's most austere desert wilderness. The utterly raw, barren mountains are of pink, red, yellow, purple, or brown rock formations. Others are grim gray or black rock. The awesome volcanic Black Mountains or the stark, eroded ranges bordering Iceberg Canyon contrast with the clear, sparkling blue waters of the reservoir. Such country is seldom visited by man, and looks as though it were inhabited by little more than rattlesnakes, lizards, and a few scattered bighorn sheep. In summer it becomes a baking inferno.

I wouldn't for a moment attempt to glamorize the Lake Mead area, but there is something very compelling about the huge body of intensely blue water surrounded by desolate, raw desert.

Between the north arm of Lake Mead and the bold escarpment of the Grand Wash Cliffs to the east sprawls one of the densest forests of Joshua trees in the Mojave Desert. Farther east the Colorado River winds through the vast chasm of the Grand Canyon, exposing a tremendous geological record of the earth's history.

Far up the canyon at the lower, warmer, and drier elevations, Mojave Desert conditions prevail. Honey mesquite forms dense thickets of greenery just above the river level in the lower stretch of the Inner Gorge. Catclaw acacia, desert willow, creosote bush, ocotillo, yucca, slender-stalked agaves, nolina, white bur sage, ephedra, and barrel, hedgehog, and prickly pear cacti grow on talus slopes and level plateaus within the canyon. Crimson Indian paintbrush, orange desert mallow, yellow desert plume, brittlebush, blue larkspur, pale lavender mariposa lily, and blue phacelia brighten the canyon in spring.

There are pinkish-colored Grand Canyon rattlesnakes, chuckwallas, and other lizards. Even a few desert bighorn sheep find the solitude they need along a precipitous stretch of isolated rock terraces deep within the Canyon. There they live undisturbed by man, hemmed in by sheer cliffs below the eastern rim of Great Thumb Mesa, two thousand feet above the river. It seems hard to believe that this secret enclave is only about thirty miles in a straight line from the South Rim's tourist-crowded Grand Canyon Village, but that is just another of the many startling contrasts of the Mojave Desert.

Lost Lakes and Living Marshes

The Great Basin Desert

A column of fragrant woodsmoke drifts through a grove of quaking aspens, a slight breeze flutters their gold leaves, and bright sunshine casts a warm glow across our campsite. Here at nearly four thousand feet above the surrounding expanses of sagebrush desert, the mid-September air is crisp and invigorating. Aspens and a few tall, stately Engelmann spruces frame a small mountain meadow where colorful wildflowers bloom in summer and mule deer come at dawn and dusk. A narrow stream sparkles in its meanderings around patches of green moss and little clumps of symmetrical young spruces.

High above this tranquil scene, the curving, splintered cirque cliffs of Wheeler Peak thrust far above timberline to look down on the dry beds of vanished lakes that form the floor of the vast mountain-enclosed expanse of the Great Basin Desert.

From the end of the paved road, trails lead into the heart of the wilderness. Groves of tall pines and spruces shade the way to crystal-clear alpine lakes. The small, tree-rimmed mirror-surfaces reflect the sheer gray cliffs and crags of the great peak that looms three thousand feet above. In the right light, the lake water takes on an emerald hue. At this utterly peaceful place the silence of an autumn day is broken only by occasional calls of a Clark's nutcracker, a raven, or a Steller's jay, or the chattering of mountain chickadees, nuthatches, and crossbills.

The trail continues around a steep ridge through a stand of tall spruces and limber pines and emerges into a very rocky, open area. Suddenly you begin spotting incredibly ancient, weather-beaten trees that add abstract, angular patterns to the wild, subalpine landscape. This is one of two main groves of the bristlecone pine (*Pinus longaeva*)—the world's oldest known living tree species. (In 1970 botanical research revealed that what had previously been considered a single species of bristlecone pine (*P. aristata*) is actually two species: *P. longaeva* in the Great Basin ranges, and *P. aristata* of the Rockies. Significant differences apparently occur in the structure of cones and needles.)

The trail switchbacks up a boulder-covered slope just below timberline, entering a magnificent grove of these venerable pines that often seem more dead than alive. On some of them only a branch or two are living, their twigs densely covered like bottlebrushes with short needles. A pair of large bristle-bracted female cones grow here and there amid the bright greenery.

Most amazing is the fact that only a narrow strip of bark may connect the living branches of the bristlecone to its roots. The rest of the massive, gnarled trunk presents an artistically grained pattern, the gray and brownish-orange wood smoothed and polished by centuries of blizzards and windstorms that engulf this exposed high country.

It is a fascinating paradox that the oldest bristlecones—the really grand old monarchs—exist in the meanest places. They have grown slowly over the centuries, enduring the hardship of this severe environment of pounding storms, dry subalpine atmosphere, rocky ground, and short growing seasons. Some trees add a mere inch or less to their trunk's diameter in a century. This has produced a very hard, dense, and extremely resinous wood that resists disease, insect invasions, fungus growth, and decay. Even a tree that died centuries ago may still be standing, the bare branches etched beautifully against the sky.

It is difficult to comprehend the age of these pines, the most ancient of which date back from three thousand to five thousand years ago. The oldest known tree, growing high in the White Mountains of eastern California, has been alive for more than 4600 years. A 4900-year-old veteran at Wheeler Peak was inadvertently cut down a few years ago. To put these figures in human terms, they mean that many bristlecone pines living today were seedlings or young trees way back when the Egyptians were building their great pyramids, and that the classical Greek and Roman civilizations and the entire history of Christianity have occurred within the lifespans of these great trees. It is something to contemplate as you walk among them.

From the bristlecones, the trail leads on above timberline to an ice field—a glacial remnant in the cold shadow of the peak's imposing cirque wall. Beneath this patch of snow and ice you can hear the eerie, muffled sound of rushing water that is the beginning of one of many delightful streams that dash down from the heights of the Snake Range. In summer their banks, at lower elevations, are bordered with yellow violets, orchids, tall purplish-blue larkspur, and bright blue lupines.

In the next mountain valley south, another stream flows from a long, narrow pond nestling right at the base of the great sweeping headwall and rocky talus slope of Baker Cirque. Far downstream, the creek has been dammed by beavers, where groves of tall aspen trees provide material for their clever engineering.

The high country also provides spectacular views far to the east and west, across the corrugated basin-and-range topography characteristic of the Great Basin. A mile and a half below the arctic-alpine tundra of the peak are the arid valleys where typical high-desert shrubs grow—the pungent, gray-leafed sagebrush (*Artemisia tridentata*) and grayish shadscale (*Atriplex confertifolia*). Bright green greasewood (*Sarcobatus vermiculatus*) is a reliable indicator of groundwater beneath extensive valley flats of clay and salt-encrusted playas.

Where the sagebrush grades into the pygmy forest of junipers and piñons at the eastern base of the mountain peak, a limestone cave is still being created by a slow but steady seepage of underground water.

Here and there, pools of water magically reflect the stalactites, stalagmites, and fluted columns. The sound of dripping water emphasizes the sense of mystery. Lacy aragonite crystals, oddly twisting helictites, and sparkling nodules of calcite delicately decorate parts of the cave's walls, ceiling, and larger formations. And there are lots of gracefully curving draperies and fluted shields—forms that are rarely found in limestone caves.

Like the aspen groves, the ancient bristlecones, and the alpine lakes high above, the myriad formations in the cool, damp depths of Lehman Caves provide an exciting contrast to the surrounding sagebrush desert.

As you travel through the long expanses of valleys and mountain ranges of the Great Basin Desert, you come now and then upon vast barren playas of cracked, curled mud, or glaring white salt flats—places where little or no plant life can grow. Along the lower slopes of arid mountains, you can sometimes see faintly parallel markings that look as though waves once lapped along the land there.

Gradually you begin to realize that in some far distant age the desert was not desert but a lush land filled with huge lakes stretching for hundreds of miles between and around the rugged ranges. The salty playas are the beds of those ancient inland seas, and the markings along the mountainsides are former shorelines.

According to geological calculations, the Great Basin was the scene of gradually expanding and contracting lakes—more than a hundred have been mapped—that coincided with four major advances and withdrawals of the Pleistocene Ice Age. These occurred roughly from a million down to about fifteen thousand years ago. The two largest of the many lakes created during those periods of increased precipitation were what geologists have named Lake Bonneville in northwestern Utah, and Lake Lahontan in northwestern Nevada.

Great Salt Lake, Utah, is a million-acre remnant of the once great Bonneville. This Ice Age lake covered more than twelve million acres—an area equal to two-thirds the size of the State of Maine or the Republic of Austria, or roughly equal to one-fourth the area of Utah. As indicated by old shoreline marks, its highest level was a thousand feet above the present lake. It then had an outlet—northward into the Columbia River basin. A vast part of the old lake bed is Great Salt Lake Desert—the largest salt flat in the desert. It lies just west of Great Salt Lake, and its seemingly endless, glaring white expanse extends impressively for about forty miles east and west, and a hundred miles north and south.

Great Salt Lake has long been famous for its briny content. With nearly ten times the proportion of dissolved salts of the oceans, the water supports swimmers with ease. Recent reports indicate, though, that an increasing inflow of freshwater from several rivers has been reducing the salinity during the past ten years and raising the level of the lake. The rising tide is, in turn, invading and destroying much of the adjacent freshwater marshland.

The lake itself is one of the most important waterfowl oases of the Great Basin. Near the northeast shore, where Bear River enters the lake, in good years a million ducks wing south in autumn from the breeding areas of Alaska and Canada. They gather in the diked marshes of cattails and bulrushes, and on the expanses of open water. Even in summer I have counted more species of birds here in a single day than I've seen at any other inland area in the United States.

Against the scenic backdrop of the snow-capped Wasatch Mountains to the east, thousands of whistling swans, Canada and snow geese, and an abundance of ducks and shorebirds fill the air and cover the water with constant movement and sound. Flocks of white pelicans, rising from nests on islands out in the lake, gracefully wheel and soar on black-tipped white wings.

Waterfowl survival has been a major issue at Bear River since the early decades of this century. After years in which agricultural irrigation drew off increasing quantities of water from Bear River, extensive mud flats became exposed or were covered with only shallow water that fluctuated with the seasons. On alkaline flats, these conditions can cause the outbreak of botulism that is fatal to water-fowl.

A bird refuge was established at Bear River in 1928. After the loss of nearly a quarter of a million birds in 1932, water-control dikes and a research laboratory were established there to study and combat the spread of botulism among the waterfowl. Progress has been made over the years, but research is continuing in the hope of finding better methods of botulism control at Bear River and other marshlands throughout the arid regions of the West.

The once-vast Lake Lahontan covered more than five million acres of northwest Nevada and a little of northeastern California. Prominent remnants of that great inland sea are Pyramid Lake, Walker Lake, and the Stillwater marshes, in Nevada; and Honey Lake just over the line in California.

Pyramid, a few miles northeast of Reno, lies almost mirage-like, extending for about thirty miles, between the Virginia and Lake ranges. Against the neutral gray-brown tones of the surrounding desert, the water is usually a striking deep blue, although at times it becomes greenish turquoise—a color produced by increases in the populations of algae and tiny crustaceans. Weird, whitish formations of calcium carbonate, called tufa, are scattered along or above the shore. Along the northwest end of the lake great conical, sharp-pointed pinnacles, known as the Needles, rise ghost-like out of the shallows and mud flats.

The name of the lake was inspired by a gigantic pyramid-shaped rock that rises abruptly more than 360 feet above the water, close to the eastern shore. Nearby is the lake's only island, a treeless, rocky place called Anaho. Although only 750 acres in area, it is such an important breeding place for white pelicans that it has been made a national wildlife refuge to protect what may be the largest of the half dozen breeding sites for this species in western North America. It is estimated that in summer between seven thousand and eight thousand of them come to Anaho Island to raise their young. Because nesting activity is so easily disrupted by man, the island is closed to all but specifically authorized visitors.

The lake is within an Indian reservation that is home to a band of the Northern Paiutes. These people were known as the Kuyuidokado, meaning the cui-ui eaters. The cui-ui is an endemic large species of sucker fish (*Chasmistes cujus*) that once ranged widely throughout Lake Lahontan but is now a unique relic of the Pleistocene, found only in Pyramid Lake.

We once spent a day at the northern part of Pyramid, near the great cluster of pinnacles. From the end of a rough dirt road we began walking across the desert scrub and onto the cracked mud flats, toward the towering formations. We had thought the walk over and back would take only an hour or so, but distances and sizes of objects in the desert are often deceptive. More than two hours later we reached the nearest gigantic formation. The irregularly tapered rock, by the water's edge, was reminiscent, on a small scale, of Mont-Saint-Michel off the coast of France.

As the sun went down behind the Virginia Mountains that evening, the colors of the lake and surrounding desert slowly softened. The scene took on a serene, mystical quality in the gathering dusk.

As the stars began to appear and grow brighter, there wasn't a sound; there wasn't even a breeze. Time seemed to be suspended—a feeling you often get in the desert.

Just a few miles northeast of the pleasant agricultural community of Fallon sprawls the largest freshwater marsh in the Great Basin Desert of Nevada. Located in the Carson Sink, in what was apparently the largest expanse of Lake Lahontan ages ago, Stillwater today is a vast stretch of diked ponds, marshland, greasewood-and-saltbush desert, and salt flats. The flats are bordered by the strange leafless, rubbery, cylindrical-stemmed pickleweed (*Allenrolfea occidentalis*). This extremely salt-tolerant plant is normally green in summer, but in autumn it makes a beautiful contrast of red against the white and grayish expanses of the playas.

Water levels of the refuge ponds are carefully regulated to provide as much open water and marsh habitat as possible, depending upon the weather and water allotments from an agricultural irrigation project. In years of sufficient water several thousand ducks stop here in March and April on their northward migration. Other concentrations of ducks, along with grebes, herons, ibises, Canada geese, plovers, phalaropes, avocets, and stilts, raise their young here during the summer.

The most impressive nesting species of these marshes is the white pelican. Flotillas of them swim about on the ponds, grabbing fish with their large orange beaks. Flocks circle overhead in V formations, flapping and gliding in sequence or in unison.

The major migration influx occurs from August to November, when nearly a quarter of a million ducks, including canvasbacks, pintails, shovelers, and green-winged teal, fly in from the north. The graceful whistling swan is the major attraction in winter, when eight or ten thousand of these beautiful white birds are here.

On a calm October evening at Stillwater, a little flock of dowitchers foraged with their long straight bills in the shallow water, while surrounding bulrushes and the barren Stillwater Mountains to the east turned brilliant orange. In the opposite direction, looking toward the setting sun, sharply silhouetted low bands of marshland, distant mountains, and a scattering of waterfowl were suspended between the golden glow of sky and mirrored water, like a scene in a magnificent Oriental painting.

In the high desert of southeastern Oregon, thirty miles south of Burns, the fluctuating marshy lakes of the Malheur region provide one of the most important sanctuaries for migrating and nesting waterfowl along the Pacific Flyway. South of these lakes in the scenic, narrow valley of the Blitzen River are irrigated meadows, ponds, marshes, and willow thickets. The river is bordered much of the way by low rims of dark basaltic rock. Beyond this valley are expanses of juniper-dotted sagebrush plains and patches of greasewood-covered alkali flats.

The spring waterfowl migrations reach their peak in early spring with spectacular concentrations of snow geese, along with Canada and Ross's geese; pintails, green-winged teal, and canvasbacks; whistling swans; and greater sandhill cranes.

In late March and early April the sandhills gather on the meadows of Blitzen Valley for their incredible dawn courtship dance. Suddenly a number of these tall gray birds begin to bob their heads and leap wildly into the air. Flapping their wings, they turn around this way and that and bound over one another. As the tempo increases, the frenzied birds utter loud, deep, guttural calls and croaks. The entire scene, in the cold half light, seems like something out of the prehistoric past.

Another early springtime sunrise drama is the courtship ritual of the sage grouse (*Centrocercus urophasianus*)—a typical bird of the sagebrush desert, and the largest American grouse. Near the southern end of the refuge, the males perform to their harems of hens gathered on the strutting grounds. The deep popping sound of their call is caused by the sudden release of air from yellowish neck sacs half hidden within their white breast feathers. It carries great distances across the plains. With their sharp tail feathers quivering and upspread like a fan, the dominant cocks strut about, uttering low guttural sounds and deflating their air sacs with a *plop*, as they compete for the largest share of hens.

By late spring cranes and grouse are nesting, snow geese and the other migrants have gone on to breeding grounds far to the north, and a tremendous influx of summer breeding birds pours into the refuge. Thousands of gadwalls, cinnamon teals, mallards, redheads, ruddy ducks, as well as herons, egrets, grebes, terns, and other shorebirds, fill the expanses of bulrushes, cattails, and open water of

Malheur Lake and Blitzen Valley. The bird migrations in autumn, although generally less impressive than those in spring, are best from late August through mid-October.

Looming on the horizon to the southeast of Malheur is the prominent volcanic fault-block plateau called Steens Mountain. Rising a mile above the surrounding desert and 9700 feet above sea level, it is reached by a dusty loop road from the southern end of Blitzen Valley. Five U-shaped gorges were carved in the mountain by tongues of Ice Age glaciers. Hiking or horseback riding trails climb steeply into these hidden places where there are sparkling streams, waterfalls, and groves of quaking aspens.

Most of Steens is covered with sagebrush, grass, and a few old gnarled junipers. From the flat summit you can look far to the east—across the broad white playa of Alvord Desert and on toward the Owyhee Desert beyond the Oregon–Idaho border. There the Owyhee River has carved a deep, colorful gorge through the wilderness.

The drive from Winnemucca, across mile after vast mile of northwest Nevada, is lonely and unspoiled. Long ranges of mountains hem in wide valleys carpeted with shadscale and sagebrush, and the pungent fragrance drifts across the desert.

We paused for a steak dinner at the tiny crossroads settlement of Denio and continued north-westward. This timeless expanse of high desert wilderness is a corner of America that seems to have remained virtually unchanged since before the coming of the white man. A gray carpet of sagebrush stretches off in all directions, interrupted only by black lava rock ridges and mesas.

We looked everywhere for a herd of the pronghorn antelope (*Antilocapra americana*), but the nearest we came was the painting of one on the entrance sign to the Charles Sheldon Antelope Range. Either they were far back from the highway, or they blend too well into the landscape. We spotted a small group of wild burros with a young one, but not another living thing. Late-afternoon sun was casting long dark shadows, and the feeling of utter remoteness could not have been more complete.

The high lava-flow plateaus extended on into Oregon, and a few miles from the state line the road dropped into Warner Valley. In the gold light of sunset, flock after flock of Canada geese winged in V formations overhead, filling the air with their honking chorus. Far up the long valley loomed the great flat-topped plateau called Hart Mountain, purple and mysterious, its contours outlined by the faint pink highlights cast by the final rays of the setting sun.

On an earlier visit to the mountain, during the August pronghorn season, we had seen not a single one of these fleet-footed animals. Now it was late September, and as we started out again in the morning, heading toward the Hart Mountain National Antelope Refuge, we hoped for better luck.

The road from the lumber-milling town of Lakeview took us back the few miles through the rolling ponderosa pine country so typical of the eastern foothills of the Oregon Cascades. Abruptly we were out of the forest and back on the high desert. The road wound down through the Lombardy poplars and neat farms of the village of Plush and skirted a large, shallow lake. We bumped along for miles on a gravel road that followed the base of Hart Mountain's gigantic lava-rock escarpment. Where intimate little canyons cut into the face of the cliff, pockets of aspens and other trees found a slightly damper, cooler environment.

The road climbed steeply among black basalt boulders and gray sagebrush. The higher we went, the more dramatic became the sweeping panorama of the series of beautiful, brim-full blue lakes strung out along the base of the great rimrock mountain. These intermittent desert lakes—Bluejoint, Stone Corral, Upper and Lower Campbell, and others toward the south—are dry, or nearly so, about three years out of ten, depending upon the whimsical pattern of precipitation.

Hart Mountain is actually a giant fault-block range, steeply uplifted along the western escarpment and gently sloping downward for many miles to the east. In this lonely sagebrush country one of the largest pronghorn herds in the country spends the spring, summer, and autumn. Only a few winter at this higher elevation, many of them migrating southward into the Sheldon refuge.

We drove on across the flat, grayish expanse of the plateau. A scattered line of thirty or forty tan-and-white pronghorns suddenly materialized, visible, yet almost camouflaged by their surroundings. A telephoto lens brought them closer, and we could see their trim, clean-cut features—long, narrow white-and-brown heads, small angular black horns, and white flanks and rumps.

A hundred yards of cautious stalking toward them was all the encroachment they would tolerate.

44

After an initial curiosity, they began gracefully moving away—loping, stopping to look back, and loping along again, until they blended like a mirage back into the landscape.

We saw three herds during the morning. Although all were at a distance, they gave us an inkling of what it must have been like in a time when millions of pronghorns are believed to have roamed across the western plains and desert valleys. Like the bison, the pronghorns were nearly wiped out by the ruthless slaughter of early settlers and explorers. Early in the twentieth century only a few thousand survived in the American West, some in small herds in the high desert country of southern Oregon and northern Nevada. Their numbers began to increase again when large parts of the summer and winter ranges were gradually brought under federal protection, during the 1920s and 1930s, in the Hart Mountain and Charles Sheldon refuges.

The protected habitat of the pronghorns is shared by many other desert animals. Nearly 150 kinds of birds have been recorded at Hart Mountain, where one of the most common and spectacular visitors is the sage grouse. There are coyotes, jackrabbits, kangaroo rats, bobcats, and mule deer as well. Bighorn sheep were wiped out here in the late 1800s, but the California bighorn (*Ovis canadensis californiana*) has been successfully re-introduced. Today a few are occasionally seen in the more remote, high elevations and along the rimrock of the escarpment.

The Sculptured Plateau

The Painted Desert

A bold, banded escarpment, the Palisades of the Desert, hems in the Grand Canyon at its far eastern end where the ribbon of the Colorado River makes a great swing from south to west. Eastward from its brink stretches the broad, sculptured plateau of the Painted Desert—a region of eroded clay badlands, petrified logs, deep canyons, flat-topped mesas, and giant red buttes. Most of this high desert of northeastern Arizona is the homeland of the Navajo and Hopi Indians.

The long, meandering gorge of the Little Colorado River cuts deeply into the flat, grassy plain just east of the Grand Canyon. Although it lacks the awesome distances of the broader canyon, the Little Colorado gorge is breathtaking. Its narrow width drops straight down—more than three thousand feet from rim to river along its deepest stretch. Sheer walls have been carved by the river through yellowish-brown, horizontally bedded limestone strata of the Kaibab and Toroweap formations that were laid down beneath a shallow sea during the Permian period, some 250 million years ago. Pre-dinosaur reptiles were then beginning to rise to dominance among the creatures on earth.

Below those strata the river has cut on through older sandstones, shales, massive cliffs of Redwall limestone, and down through the half-billion-year-old Tapeats Formation.

The silt-laden waters of this tributary stream may have taken some seven million years to grind their way down through the 275- to 300-million-years' worth of sedimentary rocks.

Even without really comprehending such vastnesses of geologic time, it is astounding to look down into the shadowed depths of the winding gorge and out across the vast grassy plateau toward distant mesas and mountains.

East of the gorge, the land drops away to the weirdly eroded shale and clay hills of the Painted Desert. The rolling landscape extends south and east, up the valley of the Little Colorado and its tributaries, to the Petrified Forest.

The subtle beauty of the Painted Desert badlands varies with the changing moods of weather and light. Cone-shaped hills, jagged ridges, small mesas and buttes capped with more resistant layers of sandstone or shale, gullied amphitheaters and escarpments, narrow ravines, and broad valleys are all displayed in infinite gradations of form and color.

During the flat light of midday, the sculptured features lose most of their definition, and the land looks bleak and barren. But the slanting rays of the sun in early morning and late afternoon dramatically accentuate the forms and texture and enliven the landscape's variegated shades of maroon, pink, red, yellow, purple, blue, brown, gray, and white. When puffy white clouds cast shadows across the land, the colors in the sunlit places seem, by contrast, even more intense. The Painted Desert can be awesomely silent, but there are times when fierce winds blow a gale, and torrential rains from violent summer thunderstorms produce flash floods that continually remold the face of the land. The Chinle Formation of the badlands is comprised of thin layers of gravel, shale, and sandstone that are interbedded with thicker layers of a clay-like material known as bentonite, a volcanic ash that was deposited under water. Although it is hard and cracked when dry and sun-baked, bentonite softens and erodes easily when wet. In its pure form, it is white or gray. The amazing range of colors has been caused largely by iron-and-manganese-oxide staining.

The Petrified Forest is a desert area where great logs and fragments of petrified wood have been eroded out of the ground. Most of these logs were once trees of several long-extinct cone-bearing species. They date back to a lush, semitropical, reptile-dominated world of the Triassic period, some two hundred million years ago. These *Araucarioxylons* apparently were related to or much like today's Norfolk Island pine of the South Pacific and the South American monkey puzzle pine.

The logs became petrified, or silicified, by being completely covered by water and sediments in an ancient marsh along a river floodplain. Where oxygen and living organisms could not break down

46

the wood, the organic matter was very gradually, atom by atom, replaced by silica, in the mysterious process called metasomatosis. Minute quartz crystals filled the cells and other spaces. Ultimately the wood was converted—to agate, onyx, opal, jasper, carnelian, or amethyst—often in a nearly perfect reproduction of the original wood structure. The exquisite patterns and shades of red, orange, yellow, purple, blue, and brown were created by oxides of iron and manganese.

These colorful trees of stone lived in a vastly different world millions of years before man came into being. As evidenced by fossil records, it was a world of tree ferns, tall pines, horsetails, and many kinds of amphibians and reptiles. A crocodile-like animal, the phytosaur, and an early, relatively small dinosaur that measured only eight feet long were notably abundant.

Today's arid, high desert environment supports very different flora and fauna—grasses, yuccas, yellow-flowered mariposa lilies, a few cacti, and ephedra; and coyote, bobcat, fox, jackrabbit, and kangaroo rat.

Rainbow, Crystal, Jasper, and Black forests are names given to some of the best areas of exposed petrified wood. In 1906 President Theodore Roosevelt proclaimed the area a national monument, believing it would end the widespread vandalism that had begun in the 1890s. In spite of fines and penalties, the looting by visitors continues. Officials estimate that some twelve tons of petrified wood are hauled out of the park annually. At this rate, it is hard to believe that very much will remain for the future.

As the sun comes up behind the giant, flat-topped, sheer-sided Mitten Buttes, sharply silhouetted against the bright eastern sky, a narrow column of woodsmoke drifts from a tiny Navajo hogan far across the desert. Flaming sunlight floods the tops of other thousand-foot-high red sandstone buttes, columns, and mesas around us. Not a sound breaks the stillness. Not a living thing moves in the hush of dawn.

The warm light works its way down the sheer cliffs and massive, outspreading alluvial pediments. It skims across the red earth of the surrounding vast desert plain that is covered here and there with small mounds of reddish-orange wind-rippled sand dunes; clumps of a low-growing, narrow-leaved yucca and prickly pear cactus; olive-green leafless ephedra; gray shadscale and saltbush; and other high-desert shrubs. An old gnarled juniper makes a striking angular pattern against the sky.

Monument Valley is an unbelievably beautiful place. Swept by fierce winds and sandstorms or baking under a scalding summer sun, covered with a mantle of heavy snow or painted with wildflowers, at all times it is awesome and magnificent.

Dominating the land are huge, monumental rock formations, widely spaced across the desert floor. These remnants of once-continuous layers of Wingate sandstone were laid down as great thicknesses of sand dunes over a vast region during the extremely arid Jurassic period, some 180 million years ago. This is the same formation that creates the massive cliffs of Canyonlands National Park to the north in Utah. Much of that ancient desert of blowing sands may have been similar to the vast accumulations of dunes in Saudi Arabia or North Africa, at a time when huge dinosaurs had become the dominant animals of the world and the very earliest mammals were just appearing.

Constantly changing light creates varying colors and moods in Monument Valley. Early-morning shadows sidelight the creviced sculpturing of the cliffs. Shadows recede and the rich red tones lose some of their brilliance as the sun rises high overhead. Wind shrouds the buttes and mesas in a dusty haze of mystery. In late afternoon the sun floods the desert with a molten orange glow, or, breaking through clouds, it dramatically spotlights individual buttes. Sunset shadows extend for many miles across the desert floor. Slowly the vibrant colors and black shadows soften and fade, and the distant profiles of the rocks take on deep purple hues. Night descends as silently as the day began.

The desert is immense, lonely, yet totally alive . . . a place of space and timelessness.

THE PLATES

(*Continued on page 113*)

2

3

4

5   6

7

8

15   16

28   30

29

37

36   38

40

41

42

43

45

44

48

49   50

53

52

57

58 59

60

61

65

66

67

(*Continued from page 48*)

37 Orange-flowered prickly pear cactus.
38 Yellow-flowered prickly pear cactus.
39 Mexican golden barrel and old-man cacti.
40 Joshua tree in the Mojave Desert.
41 Teddy bear cholla cactus in the Pinto Basin, Joshua Tree National Monument.
42 Late-afternoon shadows among the Jumbo Rocks, Joshua Tree National Monument.
43 A desert bighorn sheep.
44 Prehistoric Indian petroglyphs in the Valley of Fire State Park, Nevada.
45 Small sandstone arch in the Valley of Fire.
46 Lone Pine Peak from the Alabama Hills, Owens Valley, California.
47 Sunrise on the Sierra Nevada, with Mount Whitney set back just right of center and Lone Pine Peak, left.
48 The salt flats of Death Valley from Dante's View.
49 The "Devil's Cornfield"—arrowweed bushes in Death Valley.
50 Manly Beacon rises above the sculptured mud hills of ancient lake-bed deposits in Death Valley.
51 Evening shadows accentuate the flowing contours of Death Valley sand dunes.
52 High above the sagebrush of the Great Basin, September turns the aspens to gold against the gray crags of Wheeler Peak.
53 Bristlecone pine cones.
54 Ancient bristlecone pine, Wheeler Peak.
55 Eroded clay formations in Cathedral Gorge State Park.
56 Sunset transforms the Cathedral Gorge landscape.
57 White pelicans glide silently over Stillwater Marsh.
58 Ducks gather in a desert marsh.
59 Dowitchers feeding in the marsh as the setting sun casts a glow across the Stillwater Mountains.
60 Pronghorns at Hart Mountain.
61 Burros in the Charles Sheldon Antelope Range.
62 Bulrushes, tinted russet by autumn, in the marshes of Ruby Lake National Wildlife Refuge.
63 The evening sun spotlights the tufa-encrusted shoreline of Mono Lake beneath autumn storm clouds.
64 The Painted Desert, Petrified Forest National Park.
65 Hopi Indian garden patch among the dunes of northeastern Arizona.
66 Desert paintbrush.
67 Canyon of the San Juan River in southeastern Utah.
68 "The Mittens," Monument Valley, at sunrise.
69 Grand Canyon from the South Rim, late afternoon.

R
D
B

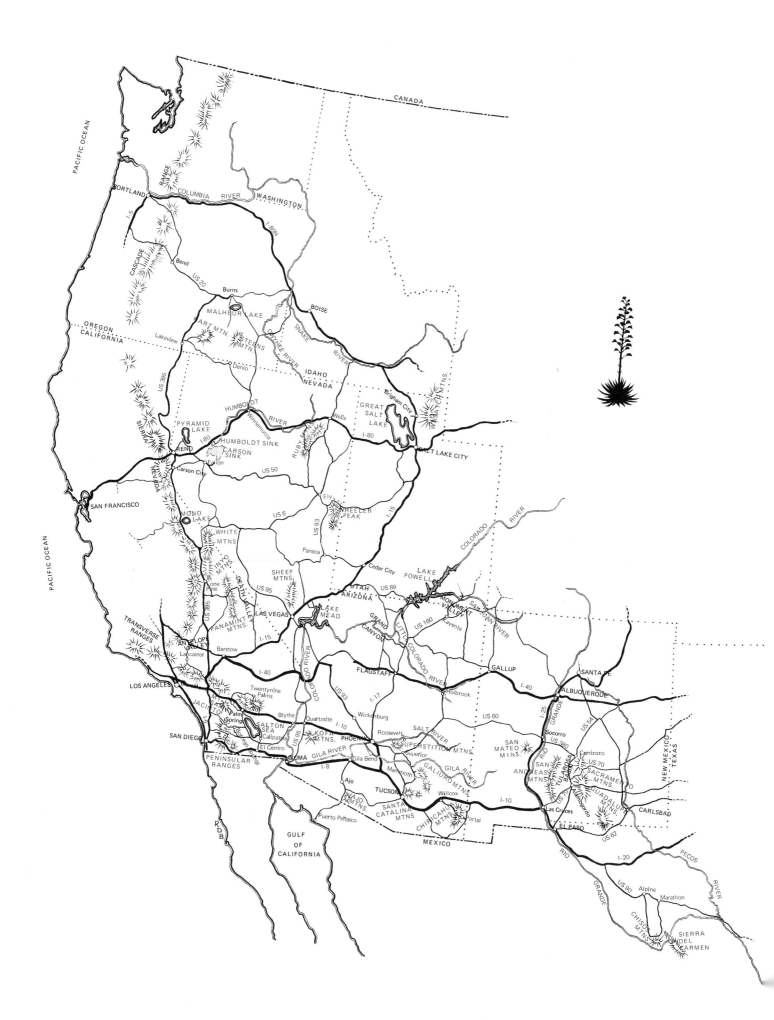

PACIFIC OCEAN

CANADA

PORTLAND
COLUMBIA RIVER
WASHINGTON
RANGE
I-5
I-80N
CASCADE
Bend
US 20
Burns
BOISE
MALHEUR LAKE
OREGON
CALIFORNIA
Lakeview
HART MTN.
STEENS MTN.
OWYHEE RIVER
SNAKE RIVER
IDAHO
NEVADA
Denio
US 395
HUMBOLDT RIVER
Winnemucca
Wells
Brigham City
WASATCH MTNS.
GREAT SALT LAKE
PYRAMID LAKE
SIERRA
I-80
HUMBOLDT SINK
CARSON SINK
Fallon
RUBY MTNS.
I-80
SALT LAKE CITY
SAN FRANCISCO
RENO
NEVADA
Carson City
US 50
US 6
ELY
WHEELER PEAK
US 93
I-15
COLORADO RIVER
MONO LAKE
WHITE MTNS.
Panaca
Cedar City
LAKE POWELL
PACIFIC OCEAN
INYO MTNS.
SHEEP MTNS.
US 95
UTAH
ARIZONA
US 89
MONUMENT VALLEY
SAN JUAN RIVER
DEATH VALLEY
Lone Pine
LAS VEGAS
LAKE MEAD
GRAND CANYON
LITTLE COLORADO RIVER
US 160
Kayenta
PANAMINT MTNS.
I-15
GALLUP
SANTA FE
TRANSVERSE RANGES
ANTELOPE VALLEY
Lancaster
Barstow
I-40
COLORADO RIVER
FLAGSTAFF
I-40
ALBUQUERQUE
LOS ANGELES
Twentynine Palms
US 93
US 17
Holbrook
I-25
RIO GRANDE
JACINTO
Indio
Palm Springs
Blythe
Quartzsite
I-10
Wickenburg
US 60
Socorro
US 380
Carrizozo
US 54
NEW MEXICO
TEXAS
SALTON SEA
Calipatria
KOFA MTNS.
PHOENIX
SALT RIVER
Roosevelt
SUPERSTITION MTNS.
SAN MATEO MTNS.
SAN ANDREAS MTNS.
US 70
SACRAMENTO MTNS.
SAN DIEGO
El Centro
US 95
YUMA
GILA RIVER
Gila Bend
Superior
GILA RIVER
GALIURO MTNS.
Mammoth
TULAROSA
Alamogordo
GUADALUPE MTNS.
PENINSULAR RANGES
I-8
Ajo
Puerto Peñasco
NAVAJO MTNS.
SANTA CATALINA MTNS.
TUCSON
Willcox
CHIRICAHUA MTNS.
Portal
I-10
Las Cruces
EL PASO
US 62
CARLSBAD
R D B
GULF OF CALIFORNIA
MEXICO
RIO GRANDE
I-20
PECOS RIVER
US 90
Alpine
Marathon
CHISOS MTNS.
SIERRA DEL CARMEN

Key to the Deserts

Chihuahuan

Arizona–Sonoran

Colorado

Mojave

Great Basin

Painted

Key to Map Numbers
1 Big Bend National Park
2 Guadalupe Mountains
      Carlsbad Caverns National Parks
3 White Sands National Monument
4 Bosque del Apache National Wildlife Refuge
5 Chiricahua Mountains
6 Saguaro National Monument
7 Aravaipa Canyon
8 Organ Pipe Cactus National Monument
9 Joshua Forest Parkway
10 Kofa Game Range

11 Algodones Dunes
12 Anza – Borrego Desert State Park
13 Joshua Tree National Monument
14 Antelope Valley
15 Owens Valley
16 Death Valley National Monument
17 Desert National Wildlife Range
18 Valley of Fire State Park
      – Lake Mead National Recreation Area
19 Grand Canyon National Park
20 Cathedral Gorge State Park
21 Wheeler Peak

22 Great Salt Lake
      – Bear River Migratory Bird Refuge
23 Ruby Lake National Wildlife Refuge
24 Pyramid Lake
25 Stillwater Marshes
26 Mono Lake
27 Malheur National Wildlife Refuge
28 Charles Sheldon Antelope Refuge
29 Hart Mountain National Antelope Refuge
30 Little Colorado Gorge
31 Petrified Forest National Park
32 Monument Valley

Parks, Monuments, Refuges, and Reservations

Within the deserts there are many places of interest that have been designated as parks, refuges, reservations, monuments, or parkways. Some are described earlier in this book, with only facts about travel information and facilities given below. Others not previously mentioned are described more fully.

Entrance fees and camping fees are charged at many of these areas. Information about fees and regulations may be obtained by writing to the addresses listed.

Chihuahuan Desert

- *Big Bend National Park* (708,000 acres): paved and back-country roads, picnic and camping areas (permit required for back-country camping), an information center, interpretive programs, groceries and service stations, and a lodge providing meals and overnight accommodations, for which reservations with National Park Concessions, Inc., are advised. Other accommodations: 103 miles north in Alpine, and 96 miles north in Marathon, on U.S. Highway 90. Boating permits required for river float trips through the canyons. Park information: Big Bend National Park, Texas 79834.
- *Guadalupe Mountains National Park* (79,000 acres), in west Texas, protects the bold, rocky southern end of a great fault-block range that rises high above salt playas, and arid creosote-bush-and-lechuguilla desert. The mountains' massive limestone strata were laid down as part of an immense reef in a shallow ocean basin more than 200 million years ago.

  Several huge gashes have been carved into this "sky island." A trail leads, from the end of a rough dirt road, into McKittrick Canyon, the walls of which rise nearly two thousand feet. In the exquisitely beautiful south fork of McKittrick there is an all-year stream, along which grow stands of chinquapin and gray oaks, walnut, velvet ash, bigtooth maple, and Texas madrone.

  Other trails climb into cool forests of pines in the high valley called The Bowl. Guadalupe Peak, at 8751 feet elevation, is the highest point in the state of Texas. The park was established in 1972, and as yet there are few facilities for visitors. A park information office is located just off U. S. Highway 62–180, 34 miles southwest of Whites City, New Mexico, and 110 miles east of El Paso, Texas. Visitors are required to register at the park office before exploring the back country. Park information: care of Superintendent, Carlsbad Caverns National Park, 3225 El Paso Road, Carlsbad, New Mexico 88220.
- *Carlsbad Caverns National Park* (46,000 acres) is a few miles northeast along Guadalupe Ridge from Guadalupe Mountains National Park, near Carlsbad, New Mexico. The enormous caverns are decorated with great domes, pillars, stalactites, and stalagmites in endless variety. The park also protects a stretch of wild, canyon-cut desert of agaves, yuccas, cacti, ocotillos, sotols, and other desert flora. A self-guiding nature trail leads from the park's paved road. To explore the wilderness back country, visitors are required to obtain a permit from the information center, at the entrance to the caverns. Overnight accommodations: in Whites City and Carlsbad, New Mexico. Park information: 3225 El Paso Road, Carlsbad, New Mexico 88220.
- *Sitting Bull Canyon and Falls* are located on the eastern slope of the Guadalupe Mountains, in the Lincoln National Forest. Drive 12 miles north from Carlsbad on U.S. Highway 285 and follow paved State Highway 137 southwest 31 miles to a right-branching 8-mile paved road to a Forest Service camping and picnic area at the road's end. A trail winds on into a narrow, sheer-walled part of the canyon, where a waterfall creates a delicate spray down the cliffs to a tiny pool. Sotols and other desert plants add to the beauty of the area. National forest information: Federal Building, 11th and New York, Alamogordo, New Mexico 88310.

- *White Sands National Monument* (140,000 acres): an 8-mile scenic drive, a picnic area, and an information center. Nearest overnight accommodations: 15 miles northeast in Alamogordo, by way of U. S. Highway 70/82. Monument information: Box 458, Alamogordo, New Mexico 88310.
- *Bosque del Apache National Wildlife Refuge* (57,000 acres): a 15-mile gravel tour road and an information booth. Nearest overnight accommodations: about 15 miles north in Socorro, by way of Interstate Highway 25. Refuge information: Box 278, San Antonio, New Mexico 87832.
- *Three Rivers Petroglyph Site* is about 17 miles north of the town of Tularosa, New Mexico, on U. S. Highway 54, where a U. S. Bureau of Land Management sign points to the 4½-mile gravel road east to a picnic area and a trail that winds up the low ridge where ancient Indian petroglyphs are carved and chipped into big boulders. Overnight accommodations: 28 miles north in Carrizozo and 30 miles south in Alamogordo.
- *Valley of Fires State Park* is 3 miles west of the town of Carrizozo, New Mexico, on U. S. Highway 380. A picnic area overlooks the vast, contorted expanse of the black lava flow, the "malpais." Overnight accommodations: in Carrizozo.
- *Chiricahua National Monument* (10,700 acres): a paved road, trails, an information center, and a camping and picnic area. Overnight accommodations: 36 miles northwest in Willcox, on Interstate Highway 10; and over the Chiricahua Mountains (road may be closed in winter) 20 miles to Portal, where reservations for lodgings are advised. Monument information: Dos Cabezas Star Route, Willcox, Arizona 85643. Other trails, and camping and picnic areas in Coronado National Forest, especially in Cave Creek Canyon, Rustler Park, Chiricahua Wilderness Area, and Rucker Canyon. Forest information: District Ranger stations in Willcox and Douglas, Arizona.

Arizona–Sonoran Desert

- *Saguaro National Monument* (77,000 acres): Rincon Mountain Unit, at eastern edge of Tucson: a 9-mile paved drive; trails, including two self-guiding nature trails; an information center; and a picnic area. A special permit is required for overnight hikes into back country. Tucson Mountain Unit, west of Tucson: a gravel road, trails, and a picnic area. Overnight accommodations: in Tucson. Monument information: Box 17210, Tucson, Arizona 85710.
- *Sabino Canyon* is located in the southern flanks of the Santa Catalina Mountains, just northeast of the city limits of Tucson, Arizona. Much of the year a clear beautiful stream flows down the rocky canyon. Willows, sycamores, and other streamside trees arch over the water, and tall saguaros grow on the talus slopes above. A trail leads a couple of miles up the canyon. Another excellent hike climbs into nearby Bear Canyon, leading to a spectacular series of seven waterfalls and pools. A Coronado National Forest information center and a picnic area are located near the entrance to the area. Overnight accommodations: in Tucson. National forest information: Box 551, Tucson, Arizona 85702.
- *Aravaipa Canyon* is an impressive gash in southern Arizona's Galiuro Mountains, through which flows a clear creek that has never been known to run dry—an unusual phenomenon in the desert. The canyon lies within the 100,000-acre Whittell Wildlife Preserve of the Defenders of Wildlife, a private organization with headquarters in Washington, D. C., and a 5000-acre U. S. Bureau of Land Management primitive area. Aravaipa is a strictly protected nature sanctuary where there are such rare birds as zone-tailed, gray, and black hawks, and two endangered species of fish: the spikedace (*Meda fulgida*) and the loach minnow (*Tiaroga cobitis*). Especially impressive is the narrow inner gorge of the canyon, above which rise the saguaro-dotted slopes and towering rocky ramparts of the mountains. Ten miles north of the town of Mammoth, Arizona, a dirt road branches from State Highway 77 and ends 11 miles to the east at a low rambling ranch house and the entrance to the reserve. A limited number of special access permits are issued to visitors by the Defenders of Wildlife's Tucson office: Third Floor, United Bank Building, 120 West Broadway.
- *Superstition Mountains,* site of the legendary Lost Dutchman Mine, rise in rugged, mysterious grandeur some thirty miles east of Phoenix, beyond Apache Junction. One interesting two-mile trail climbs along Peralta Canyon to Fremont Pass. From this vantage point, a bold 1500-foot-tall Lost Dutchman landmark, Weaver's Needle, juts up dramatically. This trail is reached east of Apache Junction by way of State Highway 80–60, and north at a Forest Service sign on Peralta Road. The trail begins at the end of this 5-mile dirt road. National Forest information: Tonto National Forest, Room 6428, Federal Building, 230 North First Avenue, Phoenix, Arizona 85025.

- *Tonto National Monument* (1120 acres), near Theodore Roosevelt Dam and Lake, protects the ruins of a two-story masonry dwelling that was built about six hundred years ago by the Salado Indians. A half-mile trail to the pueblo, from the monument's information center, climbs through typical Sonoran Desert growth of saguaro, barrel, and cholla cacti; ocotillos, jojobas, sotols, and yuccas. The monument is reached by way of State Highway 88, 3 miles southeast of the town of Roosevelt, or 30 miles northwest of Globe. Monument information: Box 707, Roosevelt, Arizona 85545.

- *Pinal Pioneer Parkway*, between Oracle Junction (25 miles north of Tucson) and Florence, Arizona, protects 30 miles of the wild Sonoran Desert along U. S. Highway 80–89. Saguaro and cholla cacti, mesquite, catclaw acacia, paloverde, and creosote bush are some of the typical plants. In spring borders of wildflowers, such as lupines, marigolds, globe mallows, and poppies, brighten the roadsides.

- *Organ Pipe Cactus National Monument* (330,000 acres): a paved highway and two gravel loop drives, an information center, a campground, and trails. Nearest overnight accommodations (reservations advised), meals, groceries, and service stations: adjacent to the monument in Lukeville, 3 miles north in Why, and 10 miles north in Ajo, on State Highway 85. Monument information: Box 38, Ajo, Arizona 85321.

- *Cabeza Prieta* (National) *Game Range* (860,000 acres) adjoins Organ Pipe Cactus National Monument to the west, and encompasses an extremely arid and wild desert area along 60 miles of the Mexican border in southwestern Arizona. About 250 desert bighorn sheep and a remnant population of the endangered Sonora pronghorn antelope live in the area. The total population of this pronghorn subspecies is estimated to number only about six hundred, a small percentage of which live in the refuge or roam across the border from Mexico. A dozen rugged and barren mountain ranges rise out of wide alluvial valleys and expanses of barren sand. Roads in the refuge are primitive, most of them passable only in four-wheel-drive vehicles. At present, visitors are not allowed to enter the area except under special circumstances, since the refuge is largely within a U. S. Air Force aerial target range. Refuge information: Box 1032, Yuma, Arizona 85364, or at the subheadquarters on State Highway 85, Ajo, Arizona. Overnight accommodations: in Ajo.

- *Kofa* (National) *Game Range* (660,000 acres) protects the magnificently splintered and spired Kofa and Castle Dome mountains and vast desert expanses where saguaro, cholla cacti, and other desert plants grow sparsely in this very arid part of western Arizona. The refuge is home for about three hundred desert bighorn sheep. Kofa's hidden Palm Canyon is one of the area's most interesting scenic spots. It is reached by way of U. S. Highway 95, about 20 miles south from the Interstate Highway 10 junction of Quartzsite, Arizona (or about 65 miles north from Yuma); then east 9 miles on a gravel road. A trail leads into the sheer-walled gorge, affording views of native fan palms in sheltered crevices high above. There are many old mines in the mountains; Kofa is a contraction of King of Arizona, the name of an extremely rich gold mine that was operated during the first decade of this century. Most of the roads in the refuge are passable only with four-wheel-drive vehicles, and visitors should inquire at the refuge headquarters (356 First Street, Yuma) before exploring the back country. Overnight accommodations: in Blythe, California, and in Yuma. Refuge information: Box 1032, Yuma, Arizona 85364.

- *Joshua Forest Parkway*, between Wickenburg and Wickieup, Arizona, on U. S. Highway 93, protects 17 miles of an unusual overlapping zone of the Sonoran and Mojave deserts, where saguaros and Joshua trees are seen growing in the same area. The Joshuas are especially striking when silhouetted against a colorful sunset.

- *Interstate Highway 10*, between Phoenix and the Colorado River at Blythe, California, provides long stretches of virtually unspoiled Sonoran Desert valleys and barren mountains. The scenery is especially impressive during the extremes of the day.

- *Interstate Highway 8*, from its junction with I–10, near Casa Grande, Arizona, westward 63 miles to Gila Bend, passes through an outstanding, wild expanse of saguaro country. From Gila Bend to Yuma, the freeway follows the Gila River Valley, steadily descending to hotter, drier, and more barren desert. There are sweeping views of raw, crumpled, volcanic mountain ranges and rock-strewn alluvial valleys, extending southward toward the Cabeza Prieta Game Range, where there is little more than the sparsest growth of creosote bush and white bur sage. Described as part of the Yuma Desert by some naturalists, and as an eastern extension of southern California's Colorado Desert by others, this is a sunburnt, lonely region, but the desolate, lunar-like landscape has its own awesome beauty.

Colorado Desert

- *Algodones Dunes*, in the extreme southeastern corner of California, were recently designated as the quarter-million-acre U. S. Bureau of Land Management's Imperial Sand Dunes Recreation Lands. They are one of the highest (some dunes are three hundred feet high) and among the most extensive sand dunes in the United States. From just a few miles west of the Colorado River, across from Yuma, Arizona, they extend northwest more than 40 miles, and average about 5 miles in width. Interstate Highway 8 cuts across the southern end, near the Mexican border, but an even more beautiful view of these yellowish-buff dunes is by way of State Highway 78, between Brawley and Glamis. The area is popular with dune-buggy enthusiasts. Overnight accommodations: in Yuma, Arizona, and Blythe and El Centro, California. Information: BLM, Federal Building, 2800 Cottage Way, Sacramento, California 95825.
- *Salton Sea National Wildlife Refuge*, at the southeastern edge of the Salton Sea, is a wintering area for great numbers of shorebirds, ducks, and geese. More than 250 species of birds have been recorded in the area. Salton Sea was formed in 1905 when the flood-swollen Colorado River burst from its channel and for two years flowed into the Imperial Valley. The refuge headquarters is reached by driving 4 miles north of the town of Calipatria, on State Highway 111, and west for 5 miles on Sinclair Road. Overnight accommodations: in El Centro and Calexico, California. Refuge information: Box 247, Calipatria, California 92233.
- *Anza-Borrego Desert State Park* (half a million acres): paved and gravel roads, back-country jeep trails, hiking trails, picnic areas, established and primitive camping areas, and information offices. Nearest overnight lodgings (reservations advised), meals, and services: Borrego Springs, surrounded by the park. Park information: Borrego Springs, California 92004.
- *Mecca Hills*, bordering Coachella Valley, just north of the Salton Sea, is another U. S. Bureau of Land Management recreation lands reserve. These hills of clay, shale, and other freshwater sedimentary formations are eroded by a number of colorful, sheer-walled gorges and canyons. Painted and Box canyons are especially beautiful. Overnight accommodations: in Indio, Palm Desert, and Palm Springs. Information: BLM, Federal Building, 2800 Cottage Way, Sacramento, California 95825.

Mojave Desert

- *Joshua Tree National Monument* (half a million acres): paved and gravel roads, trails, information centers, and camping and picnic areas. Overnight accommodations: in Twentynine Palms on State Highway 26, and Indio on Interstate Highway 10. Monument information: Box 875, Twentynine Palms, California 92277.
- *Alabama Hills* area in Owens Valley: paved and gravel roads, and a number of Inyo County and U. S. Forest Service camping and picnic areas. Trails cross the Sierra to King's Canyon and Sequoia National Parks. Other nearby accommodations: in Lone Pine, on U. S. Highway 395. Inyo National Forest information: 630 South Main Street, Lone Pine, California 93545.
- *Death Valley National Monument* (1.9 million acres): paved main roads, gravel roads and jeep trails (inquiry should be made before planning trips off paved roads, as back-country routes may be closed by storm damage), an information center, interpretive programs, camping and picnic areas, old mining town ruins, Borax Museum, groceries, service stations, meals, and overnight accommodations. Reservations advised for accommodations at Stove Pipe Wells Village and Furnace Creek Ranch and Inn. Monument information: Death Valley, California 92328.
- *Desert National Wildlife Range* (1.5 million acres): a small information center at Corn Creek Field Station, limited picnic facilities, and rough back-country roads which are not recommended for ordinary passenger vehicles. The western part of the refuge is an Air Force gunnery range, closed to visitors. Permits and reservations required for overnight camping. Overnight accommodations: in Las Vegas, about 20 miles southeast by way of U. S. Highway 95. Refuge information: 1500 North Decatur Boulevard, Las Vegas, Nevada 89108.
- *Valley of Fire State Park* (34,000 acres): paved and gravel roads, trails, an information center, and camping and picnic areas. Overnight accommodations: about 60 miles away in Las Vegas and Boulder City, and at several resorts along Lake Mead. Park information: Box 515, Overton, Nevada 89040.

- *Lake Mead National Recreation Area* (1.9 million acres): paved roads, an information center, camping and picnic areas, boat-launching ramps, and boat rentals and excursions. A number of lakeside resorts provide meals, lodgings, groceries, and service stations. Recreation Area information: 601 Nevada Highway, Boulder City, Nevada 89005.
- *Grand Canyon National Park* (1.2 million acres): paved roads, free public minibuses on South Rim (summer months), information centers, interpretive programs, and camping and picnic areas on both rims. Reservations required for camping areas below the rims. Permits required for hiking canyon trails (except the Bright Angel and Kaibab). Advance reservation required for mule trips into the canyon (Fred Harvey, Inc.). Lodgings (reservations advised with Fred Harvey, Inc., on South Rim, and TWA Services, Inc., on North Rim), meals, groceries, service stations, and other supplies. Privately conducted river boat trips on the Colorado River. Park information: Grand Canyon, Arizona 86023.

Great Basin Desert

- *Cathedral Gorge State Park* (1600 acres) is 2 miles north of the crossroads settlement of Panaca, on U. S. Highway 93, in southeastern Nevada. A delicately eroded bentonite clay escarpment borders a shallow desert valley. Gothic-like spires, fluted conical formations, and narrow, winding passageways produce a fantastic landscape. Some of the sheltered crevices provide roosts for barn owls and other birds. The ancient lake-bed deposits look grayish-brown under the full light of day. But at sunset the formations are suddenly flooded with brilliant orange light that gives them a surrealistic quality. Picnic area and small, attractive campground. Overnight accommodations: 167 miles south in Las Vegas; 118 miles north in Ely, Nevada; and about 85 miles east in Cedar City, Utah. Information: Nevada State Park System, Room 221, Nye Building, Carson City, Nevada 89701.
- *Wheeler Peak,* within the Snake Division (175,000 acres) of the Humbolt National Forest: paved and gravel roads, camping and picnic areas, trails, and a 28,000-acre scenic area. Nearest accommodations: 5 miles east in Baker. National forest information: Baker, Nevada 89311.
- *Lehman Caves National Monument* (640 acres): paved road, information center jointly with U. S. Forest Service, 1½-hour naturalist-guided tours through the caves, picnic area, restaurant (April–October). Monument information: Baker, Nevada 89311.
- *Ruby Lake National Wildlife Refuge* (37,600 acres), in northeastern Nevada, protects the extensive Ruby marshes which lie along the foot of the Ruby Mountains and are an important resting and feeding area for great numbers of migratory waterfowl. The large trumpeter swan, a species rescued from the brink of extinction some years ago at Red Rock Lakes National Wildlife Refuge in southwestern Montana, has been successfully re-introduced to a number of places throughout the Ruby Lake region. The refuge is reached (over some long stretches of gravel road): south about 75 miles from Wells, south about 60 miles from Elko, or north nearly 70 miles on a gravel road that branches north from U. S. Highway 50, about 29 miles west of Ely. Dike roads provide access across parts of the marshes. Near refuge headquarters there is a small campground on adjacent Bureau of Land Management lands. Overnight accommodations: in Elko, Wells, and Ely, Nevada. Refuge information: Ruby Valley, Nevada 89833.
- *Bear River Migratory Bird Refuge* (65,000 acres): a gravel tour route on some of the dikes, observation tower, and a picnic area. Overnight accommodations: about 15 miles east in Brigham City. Refuge information: Box 459, Brigham City, Utah 84302.
- *Pyramid Lake:* paved roads, and meals and overnight accommodations at Sutcliffe, on west shore of the lake; and 33 miles southwest in Reno.
- *Stillwater Wildlife Management Area* (143,000 acres): gravel tour route on dikes, and limited camping. Overnight accommodations: 16 miles southwest in Fallon. Refuge information: Box 592, Fallon, Nevada 89406.
- *Mono Lake,* a remnant of a much larger Ice Age lake, nestles against the eastern slope of the Sierra Nevada in California. The water is so highly saline (unusually high in boron) that little more than a tiny species of brine shrimp can live in it. Tall crags and pinnacles of calcium carbonate tufa line parts of the southern edge of the lake—a beautiful sight when late-afternoon sun shines through billowy clouds and spotlights the white, encrusted formations. Two barren volcanic islands—one of dark reddish-black cinders, and the other of white rock and sand—rise from the middle of Mono. The larger

of these contains hot springs and steam vents that bubble and hiss, and a small crater with a tiny crater lake. Gulls, terns, avocets, grebes, phalaropes, and other water birds are often attracted to the lake, and the smaller island is a U. S. Bureau of Land Management natural area to protect a nesting site for gulls. U. S. Highway 395, between Reno, Nevada, and the Owens Valley, passes between the lake and the Sierra, while the Tioga Pass road (open only in summer and early autumn) climbs dramatically from the Great Basin Desert of Mono Basin, up Lee Vining Canyon and into Yosemite National Park. Overnight accommodations: at Lee Vining, California.

- *Malheur National Wildlife Refuge* (181,000 acres): paved and gravel roads, an information center, and nearby camping areas. Overnight accommodations (reservations advised), meals, and service station at southern end of the refuge at Frenchglen. Other accommodations 32 miles north of the refuge in Burns. Refuge information: Box 113, Burns, Oregon 97720.
- *Charles Sheldon* (National) *Antelope Range* (520,000 acres) and *Sheldon National Antelope Refuge* (34,000 acres) encompass a great sweep of high sagebrush desert in northwestern Nevada—a land of mule deer and sage grouse, as well as the pronghorn. A few primitive camping areas are provided. State Highway 140 provides a paved route through the area, connecting Winnemucca, Nevada, and Lakeview, Oregon. Gravel roads lead southwest from this highway to Cedarville, California. Overnight accommodations: in Winnemucca and Denio Junction, Nevada, and in Lakeview. Refuge information: Box 111, Lakeview, Oregon 97630.
- *Hart Mountain National Antelope Refuge* (275,000 acres): gravel roads, information office, and limited primitive camping. Overnight wilderness camping by special permit from refuge headquarters. Best access by way of 19-mile paved road to Plush, and 24 miles of gravel road to refuge headquarters. Route between Malheur and Hart Mountain refuges is often very rough. Overnight accommodations: 65 miles southwest in Lakeview. Refuge information: Box 111, Lakeview, Oregon 97630.

Painted Desert

- *Little Colorado Gorge Navajo Tribal Park:* short spur road to viewpoint and picnic area, just north of State Highway 64, a few miles east of Desert View on Grand Canyon's South Rim.
- *Petrified Forest National Park* (94,000 acres): 27-mile paved, self-guiding interpretive drive between Interstate Highway 40 and U. S. Highway 180; information centers, lunch rooms, service stations, and picnic areas. Hikers required to register with park authorities, except for walks on several established short paths. The park is open only during daylight hours. Overnight accommodations: 27 miles west in Holbrook, and 21 miles east in Chambers. Park information: Holbrook, Arizona 86025.
- *Monument Valley Navajo Tribal Park* (over 1 million acres): an information center (4 miles southeast of U. S. Highway 163, near the Utah-Arizona line), a camping and picnic area, and a network of dirt roads. Conducted jeep trips from nearby towns. Reservations advised for overnight accommodations in Kayenta and Gouldings, Arizona; and Mexican Hat, Utah.
- *Goosenecks State Reserve* (10 acres) is 9 miles northwest of the town of Mexican Hat, Utah. An overlook at the end of the paved park road provides a spectacular view into the deeply incised meandering "gooseneck" canyon of the San Juan River. Picnic area. Overnight accommodations: in Mexican Hat. Park information: Utah State Division of Parks and Recreation, 1596 West North Temple, Salt Lake City, Utah 84116.

Desert Gardens and Museums

Arizona

- *Arizona–Sonora Desert Museum,* 14 miles west of Tucson, in Tucson Mountain Park. Indoor and outdoor interpretive exhibits of this living museum of fauna and flora of the Sonoran Desert of Arizona and Sonora, Mexico, provide an excellent introduction to the mysteries of desert ecology. A garden of native cacti, with clearly labeled specimens, is very helpful. (The nonprofit museum is supported largely by members and contributors.) (Admission fee.)
- *Desert Botanical Garden of Arizona,* just off East Van Buren Street in Papago Park, Phoenix. More than 3800 plants from the deserts of the world are exhibited in this well-organized 150-acre arboretum. There are 1200 cacti species, as well as other succulents, native trees, and many spring-blooming wildflowers. An annual cactus show is held in late February. (The Garden is sponsored by the nonprofit membership organization, the Arizona Cactus and Native Flora Society.) (Voluntary admission fee.)
- *Boyce Thompson Southwestern Arboretum,* 3 miles west of Superior, on U. S. Highway 60, in a scenic part of the Sonoran Desert, beneath the bold ramparts of Picket Post Mountain. Sections are devoted to cacti, to yuccas and agaves, native trees and shrubs, a riparian area, and a stretch of natural desert. The gardens attract a large variety of birdlife. Operated by the Desert Biology Station of the University of Arizona. (Small admission fee.)

California

- *Palm Springs Desert Museum,* East Tahquitz-McCallum Way, Palm Springs. Outstanding exhibits on animals and plant life, geology, climate, and Indians of the California deserts. (Small admission fee.)
- *Living Desert Reserve,* 1½ miles south of State Highway 111, on Portola Avenue, Palm Desert. From a visitor center, trails loop through this 360-acre portion of the Colorado Desert, at the northern end of the starkly eroded Santa Rosa Mountains. Much of the area consists of a broad alluvial floodplain, on which grows a spectacular "forest" of smoke trees. A small palm oasis provides a good place to see birds coming for water. (The reserve is operated as a nonprofit, membership division of the Palm Springs Desert Museum, with no admission fee.)
- *Barstow Way Station,* located just off Interstate Highway 15 on Barstow Road in Barstow, is headquarters for the U. S. Bureau of Land Management's recently established High Desert Resource Area and its staff of rangers. The station's attractive new building also provides helpful interpretive information—with exhibits on flora, fauna, archaeology, and history of the Mojave Desert in California; precautions to be observed while traveling through the desert; and information on the BLM's regulations and management policies.
- *Rancho Santa Ana Botanic Garden,* 1500 North College Avenue, Claremont. A large section of this beautiful arboretum is devoted to succulents and other desert plants. The variety of habitat provides good bird watching. (No admission charge.)
- *Huntington Botanical Gardens,* on the elegant estate of the Henry E. Huntington Library and Art Gallery, 1151 Oxford Road, San Marino. This outstanding desert garden has 25,000 specimens of desert plants of the world, including an incredible variety of fascinating shapes, sizes, and floral colors of cacti. While many species are native to the United States, a great many more are of Mexico and of Central and South America, including the massive, branched *Cereus xanthocarpus,* the beautiful golden barrels, and the white-haired old-man cactus. Other desert succulents are the varied yuccas, agaves, and South African aloes. The spectacular, tree-sized Mexican *Yucca australis,* with great pendent flower stalks, are even taller than the Joshua trees of California's Mojave Desert. (No admission fee.)

- *Santa Barbara Botanic Garden,* 1212 Mission Canyon Road, Santa Barbara. This delightful arboretum devotes a small section to more than a hundred cacti and other desert flora.

New Mexico

- *Living Desert State Park,* at the northwest edge of the city of Carlsbad, was dedicated in 1971. It presents an extensive collection of cacti and other desert flora. Exhibits of wildlife include an underground display of burrowing animals and desert reptiles. (Small admission fee.)

Caution!

The desert! . . . There were the measureless distances to narrow the eye and teach restraint; the untrodden trails, the shifting sands, the thorny brakes, the broken lava to pierce the flesh; the heights and depths, unscalable and unplumbed. And over all the sun, red and burning.

—Zane Grey
The Heritage of the Desert

Much has been written of the importance of treating the desert with respect, of avoiding foolish risks, and of traveling well prepared. Take it seriously; it is no joke. The following may help to keep you out of trouble, and in love with the desert:

- *Water.* Human survival in the desert is critically dependent upon water. The heat and extremely dry atmosphere conspire to cause rapid dehydration of the body, which in turn puts an increasing strain on the heart and other vital organs. You need from five to ten quarts of water per day when moderately active in 75- to 105-degree heat. At a walking pace in 110-degree heat, you will lose between one and two quarts of water per hour through perspiration. So be prepared. You'll never regret having too much water along.
- *Clothing.* To help curtail the loss of body moisture and to shade the body from too much direct sun, wear a broad-brimmed hat and loose-fitting, light-colored clothing. In the desert a little of that cheerful sunshine goes a long way.
- *Snakebites.* Always carry a snakebite kit, both in the car and on backpack trips, and learn ahead of time just how it works. Shock is a major danger after a snakebite. As a person under stress can more than double the influence of toxic venom, keep calm!
- *Back-country travel.* Particularly when you are exploring unpaved back roads or jeep trails, it is common sense to notify someone—a friend, a park ranger, or some other responsible person—ahead of time of your route and expected time of return. (Don't neglect to report your return, so that a needless and costly search is not made.) Some parks, such as Big Bend, require a permit

to hike into back country, to drive on unpaved roads, or to make overnight camping trips.
- *Desert equipment.* Gasoline, oil, tires, radiator, and general condition of the vehicle should certainly be checked before launching forth across the wilds of the desert. Equipment for desert driving should include such items as a reliable map, matches, flashlight, compass, extra food, water (two gallons per person per day and five gallons for the car radiator), water purification tablets, sunburn ointment, blankets or a sleeping bag (in the dry atmosphere, nights can get very cold, even when daytime temperatures are high), first-aid kit, pocketknife, pair of gloves, ax, GI shovel, tire jack, tire pump and gauge, an extra fan belt, emergency flares, a couple of sturdy plywood planks to help get out of sand traps or support the jack, and a tow chain or rope.
- *Getting stuck.* It is generally sound advice to stay with your vehicle and find shelter from the sun—beneath the car, if no other shade is available close by. Only as a last resort should you try to walk for help, unless you know help can be found nearby. If you must leave your car to go for help, be certain to take as much water as you can carry, and a hat.
- *Deceptive distances and temperatures.* Particularly for those accustomed to more humid and more closed-in environments, the vastness and clear atmosphere of the desert can be extremely

124

deceptive. Mountain ranges that seem just two or three miles away may actually be ten or twenty. A ridge that appears a half mile from you could be several miles distant. Temperatures, too, can fool you in a dry region. When a weather report forecasts 100 degrees, this refers to the air temperature in the shade. Out in the sun, the reading would be closer to 125 degrees, while the ground temperature could soar to 150, or even to 190 degrees.

• *Getting lost.* If you do become lost, remember that you can literally walk in circles unless you keep your eye on a distant landmark or use a compass. Otherwise you'll be like Pooh and Piglet in *Winnie-the-Pooh*, wandering about after "woozle" tracks.

• *Flash floods.* Beware of tidal-wave-like flash floods, caused by summer and early-autumn thunderstorms, that sweep down desert canyons and arroyos. These terrifying floods often extend for miles beyond the area of torrential rainfall.

• *Mental attitude.* Panic is a real villain. It not only leads you to act foolishly, even disastrously, but it can rob you of vital energy when it is most needed to cope with difficulties. Clear thinking is the most important prerequisite to surviving an emergency situation—easier said, of course, than done.

Further information on desert survival, such as driving techniques, getting out of soft sand, and producing water from a sun still, is available in Alan H. Siebert's *To Hell on Wheels: The Desert Mobility Manual.*

Protecting the Desert Heritage

Hot, dry, and often dusty, these lands are one of the harsher environments for earthly life. You might think they could well look after themselves. But the subtle adaptations of desert life form a fragile ecology. Tracks of off-road vehicles persist for decades. Indiscriminate road-making causes much permanent damage. This is to say nothing of the obliteration due to uncontrolled real estate development. . . . The peace and beauty of the desert and the scientific knowledge to be gained from better understanding its life forms are rich assets which only the most improvident land planner would throw away.

—*The Christian Science Monitor*
(May 19, 1972, editorial)

There are a number of private organizations helping to save the deserts. Information about them may be obtained from the following:

California Tomorrow
681 Market Street
San Francisco, California 94105

National Audubon Society
950 Third Avenue
New York, New York 10022

Desert Protective Council
Box 4294
Palm Springs, California 92262

National Parks & Conservation Association
1701 Eighteenth Street, N.W.
Washington, D.C. 20009

Environmental Defense Fund
2728 Durant Avenue
Berkeley, California 94704

Sierra Club
1050 Mills Tower
San Francisco, California 94104

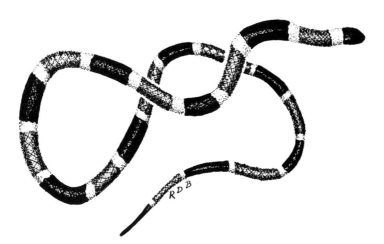

Further Reading

Abbey, Edward. *Cactus Country* (Sonoran Desert of Arizona). New York: Time-Life Books, 1973.

Ash, Sidney R., and David D. May. *Petrified Forest: The Story Behind the Scenery.* Holbrook, Arizona: Petrified Forest Museum Association, 1969.

Austin, Mary. *The Land of Little Rain.* Garden City, N.Y.: The Natural History Library, Doubleday & Company, Inc., 1962.

Benson, Lyman. *The Cacti of Arizona.* Tucson: University of Arizona Press, 1950, 1974.

Benson, Lyman, and Robert A. Darrow. *The Trees and Shrubs of the Southwestern Deserts.* Albuquerque: University of New Mexico Press, 1945, 1954.

Brown, G. W., Jr., ed. *Desert Biology,* Vol. 1. New York: Academic Press, 1968.

Butcher, Devereux. *Exploring Our National Parks and Monuments.* Boston: Houghton Mifflin Company, 1947, 1969.

————. *Our National Parks in Color.* New York: Clarkson N. Potter, 1965, 1968.

————. *Exploring Our National Wildlife Refuges.* Boston: Houghton Mifflin Company, 1955, 1963.

Chase, J. Smeaton. *California Desert Trails.* Boston: Houghton Mifflin Company, 1919.

Clements, Thomas. *Geological Story of Death Valley.* Death Valley: Death Valley 49ers, 1954, 1970.

Costello, David F. *The Desert World.* New York: Thomas Y. Crowell Company, 1972.

Dawson, E. Yale. *Cacti of California.* Berkeley: University of California Press, 1966, 1971.

Dodge, Natt N. *Flowers of the Southwest Deserts.* Globe, Arizona: Southwest Parks and Monuments Association, 1951, 1965.

————. *Organ Pipe Cactus National Monument.* Washington, D.C.: U.S. Government Printing Office, 1964.

————. *Poisonous Dwellers of the Desert.* Globe, Arizona: Southwest Parks and Monuments Association, 1968, 1974.

————. *The Natural History Story of White Sands National Monument.* Globe, Arizona: Southwest Parks and Monuments Association, 1971.

Dunbier, Roger. *The Sonoran Desert: Its Geography, Economy, and People.* Tucson: University of Arizona Press, 1968.

Earle, W. Hubert. *Cacti of the Southwest.* Phoenix: Arizona Cactus and Native Flora Society, Inc., 1963, 1973.

Gebhardt, Chuck. *Inside Death Valley.* San Jose, California: Mastergraphics, 1973.

Grey, Zane. *The Heritage of the Desert.* New York: Harper & Brothers, 1910.

Heald, Weldon F. *Sky Island* (Chiricahua Mountains). Princeton, N.J.: D. Van Nostrand Company, Inc., 1967.

Henderson, Randall. *On Desert Trails.* Los Angeles: Westernlore Press, 1961.

Jackman, E. R., and R. A. Long. *The Oregon Desert.* Caldwell, Idaho: The Caxton Printers, Ltd., 1964, 1973.

Jackson, Earl. *The Natural History Story of Chiricahua National Monument.* Globe, Arizona: Southwest Parks and Monuments Association, 1970.

Jaeger, Edmund C. *A Naturalist's Death Valley.* Death Valley: Death Valley 49ers, 1957, 1971.

————. *Desert Wildflowers.* Stanford, California: Stanford University Press, 1940, 1969.

————. *Desert Wildlife.* Stanford, California: Stanford University Press, 1961.

————. *The California Deserts.* Stanford, California: Stanford University Press, 1938, 1965.

————. *The North American Deserts.* Stanford, California: Stanford University Press, 1957, 1961.

James, George Wharton. *Wonders of the Colorado Desert* (2 vols.). Boston: Little, Brown & Company, 1906.

Kirk, Ruth. *Desert: The American Southwest.* Boston: Houghton Mifflin Company, 1973.

————. *Exploring Death Valley.* Stanford, California: Stanford University Press, 1956, 1973.

Klauber, Laurence M. *Rattlesnakes: Their*

Habits, Life Histories, and Influence on Mankind (2 vols.). Berkeley: University of California, 1956.

Krutch, Joseph Wood. *The Desert Year*. New York: William Sloan Associates, 1952.

————. *Voice of the Desert*. New York: William Sloan Associates, 1955.

Lamb, Edgar and Brian. *Colorful Cacti of the American Deserts*. New York: Macmillan Publishing Company, 1974.

Larson, Peggy. *Deserts of America*. Englewood Cliffs, N.J.: Prentice-Hall, 1970.

Lee, Bourke. *Death Valley: The Immortal Desert*. New York: Ballantine Books, 1974.

Lindsay, Diana E. *Our Historic Desert: The Story of the Anza-Borrego Desert*. San Diego: Copley Books, 1973.

Lowe, Charles H. *Arizona's Natural Environment*. Tucson: University of Arizona Press, 1964.

McDougall, W. B., and Omer E. Sperry. *Plants of Big Bend National Park*. Washington, D.C.: U.S. Government Printing Office, 1951, 1957.

Maxson, John H. *Death Valley: Origin and Scenery*. Death Valley: Death Valley Natural History Association, 1965, 1972.

Maxwell, Ross A. *The Big Bend of the Rio Grande: A Guide to the Rocks, Geologic History, and Settlers*. Austin: University of Texas Press, 1968, 1971.

Mockel, Henry R. and Beverly. *Mockel's Desert Flower Notebook*. Twentynine Palms, California, 1962, 1971 (privately published).

Munz, Philip A. *California Desert Wildflowers*. Berkeley: University of California Press, 1962, 1972.

Olin, George. *Mammals of the Southwest Deserts*. Globe, Arizona: Southwest Parks and Monuments Association, 1954, 1965.

Phillips, Allan; Joe Marshall, and Gale Monson. *The Birds of Arizona*. Tucson: University of Arizona Press, 1964.

Rickett, Harold W. *Wildflowers of the United States, Vol. 4: The Southwestern States*. New York: McGraw-Hill Book Company, 1966.

Schumacher, Genny. *Deepest Valley: Guide to Owens Valley*. San Francisco: Sierra Club, 1962.

Shelton, Napier. *Saguaro National Monument*. Washington, D.C.: U.S. Government Printing Office, 1972.

Shreve, Forrest, and Ira L. Wiggins. *Vegetation and Flora of the Sonoran Desert*. Stanford, California: Stanford University Press, 1964.

Siebert, Alan H. *To Hell on Wheels: The Desert Mobility Manual*. Pasadena, California: Brown Burro Press, 1974.

Sutton, Ann and Myron. *The Life of the Desert*. New York: McGraw-Hill Book Company, 1966.

Van Dyke, John C. *The Desert*. New York: Charles Scribner's Sons, 1901.

Venning, Frank D. *Cacti*. New York: Golden Press; Racine, Wisconsin: Western Publishing Company, 1974.

Warnock, Barton H. *Wildflowers of the Big Bend Country, Texas*. Alpine, Texas: Sul Ross University, 1970.

Wauer, Roland H. *Birds of Big Bend National Park and Vicinity*. Austin: University of Texas Press, 1973.

Wheeler, Sessions S. *The Desert Lake: The Story of Nevada's Pyramid Lake*. Caldwell, Idaho: The Caxton Printers, Ltd., 1967, 1969.

————. *The Nevada Desert*. Caldwell, Idaho: The Caxton Printers, Ltd., 1971, 1972.

Woodin, Ann. *Home Is the Desert*. New York: The Macmillan Publishing Company, 1964.